5th Annual National Conference

of

All India Association of Medical Social Work Professionals

(On the occasion of World Social Work Day)

at

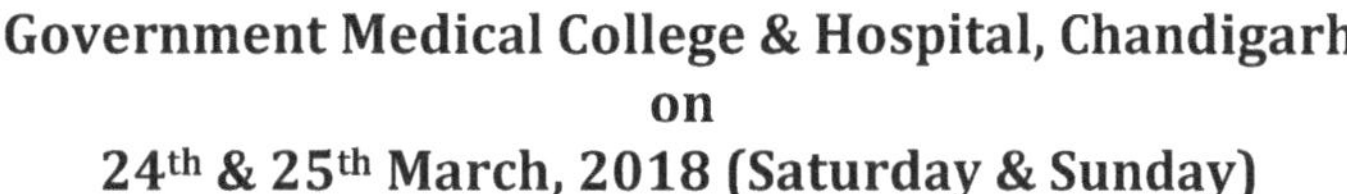

Government Medical College & Hospital, Chandigarh

on

24th & 25th March, 2018 (Saturday & Sunday)

Theme

Social Work Intervention in Health/Mental Health Setup

Organised by:

Medical Social Work Professionals,
Government Medical College & Hospital, Chandigarh

Social Work Intervention in Health/Mental Health Setup

Souvenir

5th ANNUAL NATIONAL CONFERENCE OF ALL INDIA ASSOCIATION OF MEDICAL SOCIAL WORK PROFESSIONALS

Printed at:
SANJAY PRINTERS
404, Industrial Area, Phase-II, Chandigarh, India

V.P. Singh Badnore
Governor of Punjab
and
Administrator
Union Territory, Chandigarh

Raj Bhavan
Chandigarh

Message

I

Parimal Rai, IAS

Adviser to the Administrator
Union Territory of Chandigarh
U.T. Secretariat, Sector 9
Chandigarh-160 017
Tel: 0172-2740154 (O)
Fax : 0172-2740165
Email: adviser-chd@nic.in

Message

It give me immense pleasure to recognise the positive efforts of the management of GMCH-32 in organizing the 5th annual conference of AIAMSWP on the theme "Social Work Intervention in Health/Mental Health Setup" from 24th & 25th March, 2018.

This initiative will bring together healthcare professionals, academicians, students of social studies and other professionals working in the field of medical/health set and social work from across the country on one platform for exchange of ideas, methodologies & experiences.

I am sure that this conference would be of great help in addressing various issues related to this field and will also help enhance the skills and knowledge of students. I convey my best wishes to all the participants and organizers and for the success of this conference.

16.3.18

(Parimal Rai)

Anurag Agarwal, IAS

Home Secretary,
Chandigarh Administration,
U.T. Secretariat, Sector 9
Chandigarh-160 017
Tel: 0172-2740008, 2740216 (O)
Fax : 0172-2740337
Email: hs-chd@nic.in

Message

I feel delighted to learn that GMCH-32 in organizing the 5th Annual Conference of AIAMSWP on the theme "Social Work Intervention in Health/Mental Health Setup" from 24th & 25th of this month.

This conference will serve as an enrichig platform for health care professionals, academicians, students of social studies and other professionals working in the field of medical/health setup from across the world to enhance their knowledge and skills. The wealth of experience shared by eminent professionals from this field on the theme of the conference will be a boon for all the participants.

I extend my best wishes to all the participants and organisers of this conference and wish success to the students who are working in this field.

(Anurag Agarwal)

KIRRON KHER
MEMBER OF PARLIAMENT (LOK SABHA)
CHANDIGARH
Chairperson:
Commonwealth Women Parliamentarians (CWP) Steering Committee

Member:
- Standing Committee on Home Affairs
- Consultative Committee on Skill Development & Entrepreneurship
- ICWA (Indian Council of World Affairs)

किरण खेर
सांसद (लोक सभा)

Message

It is pleased to note that Government Medical College & Hospital, Chandigarh keeps organizing various academics. This time Medical Social Work Professionals of Government Medical College & Hospital, Chandigarh are organizing a National Conference on 24th & 25th March 2018.

Human suffering with different health conditions defiantly needs more than just medicine. It is nice that the social worker disciplinary is there to take care of various social factors which have a very important role in the prevention, intervention and rehabilitation of various diseases. I hope the conference will enhance the understanding and give a new direction to it.

I wish all success to the conference.

Kirron Kher
(kirron Kher)

DAVESH MOUDGIL
MAYOR
CHANDIGARH

MUNICIPAL CORPORATION
NEW DELUXE BUILDING, SECTOR 17,
CHANDIGARH -160 017
Resi. : #138, First Floor,
Sec. 18-A,Chandigarh 160 018
Office : 0172-5021411, 5021418
Mobile: 096537-77777
E-mail: daveshmoudgil@gmail.com

Message

I am glad to know that Medical Social Work Professionals of GMCH, Chandigarh is organizing 5th annual conference on the theme "Social Work Intervention in Health/Mental Health Setup" on 24th & 25th March this year.

First off all my heartiest congratulations to all the office bearers and members of the Association who are working hard in the field of helping the people of society and the department of GMCH, Chandigarh under which association the conference is going to take place. I think its really important to de-stigmatize mental illness in any form. I think there is a lot of people that are carrying around guilt and shame and going through something, that they have has to overcome and we all especially the professionals in this field should take care of their well being.

I wish all the very best for the success of the Conference in welfare of persons with mental health & their caregivers.

(Davesh Moudgil)

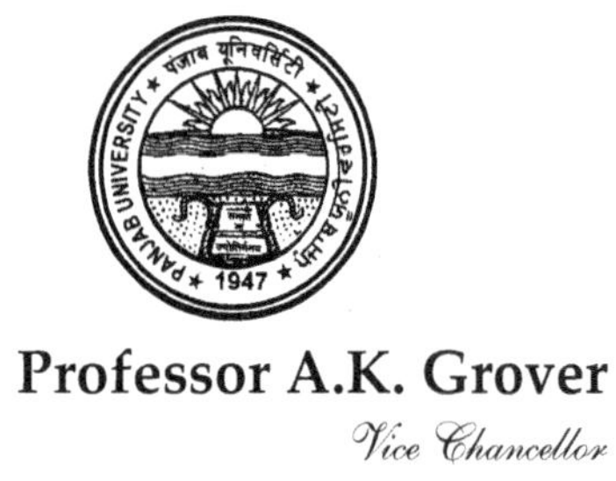

PANJAB UNIVERSITY
CHANDIGARH, India 160014

Professor A.K. Grover
Vice Chancellor

Message

I am happy to learn that the Medical Social Work Professionals of Government Medical College & Hospital, Chandigarh are organizing the 5th Annual National Conference at GMCH, Sector-32, Chandigarh from 24-25 March, 2018.

The social worker is an emerging disciplinary in the field of health and mental health in India. Social workers have a very important role in the prevention of various diseases through educating and sensitizing the community in addition to managing the treatment and rehabilitation in the hospital.

'Social Work Intervention in Health/Mental Health Setup' is an apt theme of the conference and I am sure the conference will enhance the know ledge and provide a new direction to develop the skills of Social Work Professionals in the health care setup.

I extend my best wishes to the organizers for the success of this conference.

Arun K. Grover

POSTGRADUATE INSTITUTE OF MEDICAL EDUCATION AND RESEARCH, CHANDIGARH - 160 012 (INDIA).
Phone: (Off.) 0172-2748363, 2755556, Fax: 0172-2745078,2744401
Email: dpgichd@hotmail.com Website: http://pgimer.nic.in, http://pgimer.gov.in

Dr. Jagat Ram M.S., F.A.M.S
DIRECTOR
&
Professor of Ophthalmology

Message

It gives me immense pleasure to know that the Medical Social Work Professionals of the Government Medical College and Hospital, Sector 32, Chandigarh, are organizing the 5th Annual National Conference of All India Association of Medical Social Work Professionals at the Medical College, Chandigarh on 24-25th March, 2018.

The theme "Social Work Intervention in Health/Mental Health Set up" of the Conference is relevant to the present day scenario. I am given to understand that this conference will be beneficial to all the healthcare professionals, academicians, students of social studies and other professionals working in the field of medical/mental health set up or the social work professionals. More than 200 delegates from the various institutions and universities of India are expected to participate in this conference.

My heartiest congratulations to the organizers of the Conference and best wishes for the grand success of this event.

(Jagat Ram)

Ravi Gupta
MS, DNB, FRCS, FACS, FAMS, FIMSA, FAOPA

Medical Superintendent
Professor, Orthopaedics cum
Project Director, Sports Injury Centre
Government Medical College & Hospital
Sector 32, Chandigarh-160 030

President, Indian Acad. of Arthroscopy and Sport.Med
President, Indian Society for Surgery of Hand
Chairman Ethics Committee, GMC (Mewat (Haryana)
Ex-Member Senate, Panjab University, Chandigarh
Editor in Chief: J Arthroscopy & Joint Surgery
Asstt Editor :'Indian J Orthopaedics
Member, Research Advisory Board, Swami Rama University, Dehradun
Member, Faculty of Medical Sciences, PU, Chd.
Member Board of Studies BFU Health, Punjab
Member Task Force Health & Med Edu Punjab
Member Board of Control Inst. Dental Science, PU Chd.
Chairman, Hand Section, Indian Orth Association
Former President: Punjab Orth Association

Message

It is a matter of privilege and pride for me to write this message for the upcoming Conference on the subject entitled "Social Work Intervention in Health/Mental Health Setup" being organized by All India Association of Medical Social Work Professionals. The Medical Social Workers provide an impressive array of services in the hospital setting that ranges from patient counseling, individual counseling, group discussions & other health services, and provide support to patients with serious or chronic illnesses. They act as an important link between patients and hospital services. The field of practice for professional Medical Social Worker is expanding in the hospital and is becoming challenging day by day that requires periodic enhancement of knowledge and skills of social work professionals.

Over the years, dramatic improvements have been made in the field of Medical Social Work that needs to be propagated and this Conference will enrich and update knowledge of not only delegates but also faculty, resident doctors, nurses, academicians and all other health care workers. Further, the present Conference being organized by Medical Social Workers of our institution is a step forward in this direction and is a matter of pride for GMCH.

I congratulate the organizers for taking this important plunge and wish that the forum turns out to be successful and purposeful.

10.3.18

(Prof. Ravi Gupta)

Government Medical College & Hospital, Chandigarh

Phone : 0172-2676023. Fax - 0172-2609360, 2608488

Satish Kumar Jain, HCS
Additional Director (Admn.)

Message

I am delighted to know that Medical Social Workers of Government Medical College & Hospital, Chandigarh are organizing a National Conference on 24th & 25th March, 2018.

I am happy to learn that the initiative taken by the Medical Social Workers of GMCH will bring out the best creativity and express their thoughts in the Conference.

The role of Social Workers in hospital envisages, giving help and direction to the needy patients in the complex environment. The tremendous energy put by the Social Workers in organizing the National Conference will be fruitful in bringing out the best Academic feast for everyone.

I, once again congratulate the organizers for their endeavor and wish them all the best.

15/3/18

(Satish Kumar Jain)

Dr. B.S. Chavan
MD., F.I.P.S., M.A.M.S., F.I.M.S.A., D.H.M.

Director-Principal
Government Medical College & Hospital
Sector 32, Chandigarh-160 030

Director
Govt Rehabilitation Instt. for Intellectual Disabilities,
Sector 31, Chandigarh - 160 030
Director, Mental Health Institute
Sector 32, Chandigarh - 160 030

CHANDIGARH ADMINISTRATION
Room No. 421O, Level ll,Block-D
Tel.: 0172-2655253-60 Extn. 4321
Fax : 0172-2609360
E-mail : dpgmch-chd@gmch.gov.in
drchavanbs@gmail.com
www.gmch.gov.in

Message

It gives me immense pleasure to learn that the Medical Social Work Professionals of Govt. Medical College 86 Hospital, Chandigarh, are organizing the 5th Annual National Conference on the theme 'Social Work Intervention in Health/Mental Health Set-up' on 24-25 March, 2018.

GMCH, Chandigarh, is providing State of the Art medical care for the citizens of Chandigarh and the neighbouring states. Every human being desires to have happiness, fulfillment, success, prosperity, health and bliss in life. A healthy mind and healthy thoughts can be nurtured only through positivism. If a person is happy, he can attain his chosen goals without any hurdles.

It is also appreciable that this Conference is the 5th consecutive educational programme being held by the medical social workers of GMCH, Chandigarh. Such events need to be made a regular feature for upgrading clinical skills of medical social workers working in GMCH for providing holistic medical care to the patients coming to GMCH.

I am sure that the deliberations of this conference would go a long way in benefiting the delegates. I congratulate the organizers and wish the programme a grand success.

Dr. B.S. Chavan
Chief Patron

ALL INDIA ASSOCIATION OF MEDICAL SOCIAL WORK PROFESSIONALS

Dr. Om Prakash Giri

#107, SFS DDA Flats,
Yusuf Sarai (Gulmohar Enclave),
New Delhi-110049
Secretariat:
DDTC, PGIMER, Chandigarh-160012
Web: https://aiamswp.wordpress.com
Email: gsaiamswp@gmail.com
Mobile: 09417920610

Message

My Dear Colleagues and Friends,

Greetings from the All India Association of Medical Social Work Professionals (AIAMSWP).

It gives me immense pleasure to welcome you all to the 5th Annual National Conference of the AIAMSWP, scheduled to be held at the Government Medical College & Hospital, secor-32, Chandigarh on 24-25th March, 2018 on the occasion of World Social Work Day. World Social Work Day is an international effort by the International Federation of Social Workers. World Social Work Day 2018 created another opportunity for the Social Work Professionals to enhance the knowledge and skills for better social work practices in health care. I extend my felicitations to all the participants of this National Conference. I am quite certain that under the dynamic leadership of Mr. Raghavendra Kumar Rai and Dr. Kamlesh Kumar Sahu this programme for the Social Work Professionals and other interested Health/Mental Health professionals will be a great success.

All India Association of Medical Social Work Professionals is formed at the national level dedicated for the promotion of standards and enhancement of the status of Medical Social Work Professionals in India by organising conferences, seminar and many other professional activities. It is very gratifying to see such efforts to promote its stated objectives.

I wish all the success to the National Conference of AIAMSWP.

Looking forward and waiting to meet all of you in the conference.

Thanking you with warm regards

Dr. Om Prakash Giri
General Secretary

ALL INDIA ASSOCIATION OF MEDICAL SOCIAL WORK PROFESSIONALS

Rashmi Sharma

#107, SFS DDA Flats,
Yusuf Sarai (Gulmohar Enclave),
New Delhi-110049

Message

Dear Colleagues,

I am very pleased that the Medical Social Work Professional of GMCH Chandigarh are organizing the 5th Annual National Conference of All India Association of Medical Social Work Professionals at GMCH Chandigarh on the occasion of World Social Work Day being celebrated on 20th march of this year across the world.

I hope that the conference will be an effective platform for the professionals' students and faculty members to present innovative ideas have debate and interaction to come-out with newer tool and technique to make social work profession more efficient. I wish all the success to the event.

Rashmi Sharma

(President)

ALL INDIA ASSOCIATION OF MEDICAL SOCIAL WORK PROFESSIONALS

Raghavendra Kumar Rai

Secretary,
North Zone (AIAMSWP) &
MSW, Department of Ophthalmology,
GMCH, Chandigarh
Contact: 8054434328,
Email: mswgmchprofessional@gmail.com

Message

Dear Colleagues,

It is a proud privilege for the Medical Social Work Professionals of Government Medical College and Hospital, Chandigarh to organize this event. We are eagerly looking forward to welcome you all. There is a series of enriched invited lectures, symposiums, workshop and parallel sessions in this conference. That can help us to improve the working conditions for Medical Social Work Professional and social work practices in different fields.

I am pleased to state that organizing committee of this conference has worked hard to provide a unique platform for scientific deliberations in the field of social work practices and arrangements regarding the comfort of delegates. Chandigarh is known for its Sukhna Lake, Rock Garden, Rose Garden and Mansa Devi Mandir. Also there is variety of restaurants, pubs, shopping malls and tourist places like Kasauli, Shimla, Kufri, Manali etc. nearby Chandigarh. I hope this event, hospitality and the beauty of Chandigarh would give a perfect joy to all of you.

I take this opportunity to invite you to be a part of 05th Annual National conference of All India Association of Medical Social Work Professionals to make the event a grand success.

Jai Hind

Raghavendra Kumar Rai
(Organizing Secretary)

Dr. Kamlesh Kumar Sahu
M.A, M. Phil. PSW, Ph.D
Associate Professor (PSW)

Department of Psychiatry
Government Medical College & Hospital
Sector 32, Chandigarh - 160 030
E-mail: withkamlesh@gmail.com
Mobile : 9888871120

Message

It gives us immense pleasure to welcome you all to the 5th Annual National Conference of the AIAMSWP at Government Medical College & Hospital, Chandigarh from 24th to 25th March 2018 in the 'City Beauty' Chandigarh. I hope that you would enjoy the tourist attractions present in and around our beautiful city apart from attending the enriching scientific sessions.

We must follow multidisciplinary team approach in the health or mental health care medical/psychiatric social work is an integral part of the care treatment and rehabilitation of persons with mental illness. The theme of the conference "Social Work Intervention in Health/Mental Health Setup" is very apt in the present social milieu. I am sure that the deliberations during this three days event will add some new directions to the practice and research on this model of health care.

It was a great challenge to becoming the Chairperson of the organizing committee. I am really thankful to Mr. Raghavendra Kumar Rai, the Secretary, North Zone (AIAMSWP) for his vast trust on me and given this opportunity to work and contribute for this great endeavor. I am sincerely grateful to Prof. BS Chavan who has given us this opportunity to work and contribute for such great endeavors earlier; so that I am able to take such responsibility under his patronage. This conference is the culmination of efforts of many individuals. It has been very inspiring to observe all the committees working in unison towards making this convention a great success. It was a very enriching experience while working with the colleagues for this great cause. I would like to thank each one of them for their support, affection and everything. It was very encouraging to get overwhelming response from you all; we received around 100 abstracts across the country apart from well wishes, encouragement and valuable suggestions, I am sincerely thankful for the same.

This souvenir is basically a collection of all abstracts submitted for the conference; the scientific committee particularly Mr. Prashant did a great job of compiling and editing. So, I would like to express my sincere gratitude to Mr. Atul, the chairperson scientific committee and all others for making my job easier.

I am sure, your valuable contributions have enriched this conference and it will be a memorable event for you. Looking forward to have warm interaction with you. I wish to have your comfortable and present stay at Chandigarh. I am sorry for any mistake in the souvenir or unpleasant happenings during the conference.
With warm welcome and regards

Dr. Kamlesh Kumar Sahu
Chairman Oragnising Committee

Shikha Tyagi
MSW, M.Phil. (PSW)
Assistant Professor (PSW)

Department of Psychiatry
Government Medical College & Hospital
Sector 32, Chandigarh - 160 030
E-mail: sparklingshikha@gmail.com

Message

I am glad to write the message for the 5th Annual National Conference of All India Association of Medical Social Work Professionals which is being held at Government Medical College & Hospital, Chandigarh from 24th-25th March, 2018. The theme of the conference is "Social Work Intervention in Health/Mental Health Setup ".

I am further pleased to inform you that there has been overwhelming response to this conference and we have received........scientific abstracts across the country. Such an overwhelming response is an indication that Annual National Conference of Medical Social Work Professionals is an excellent forum for professionals, researchers, academicians, and students to meet, deliberate and discuss their research experiences in the field of Social Work. The theme of the conference has been chosen so that medical social workers can share evidence based best practices and be develop and implement uniform intervention practices across all hospitals in India.

Apart from the symposium and workshops by the eminent speakers, there shall be free scientific free paper and poster presentation session by the researchers, post-graduates and undergraduate students. Like each year award sessions are also kept for motivating professionals as wells as students.

The organizing team has been working very hard for last one year to make this event memorable and make your stay comfortable during your visit to "The City Beautiful".

Looking forward to meet you all during the conference.

Shikha Tyagi

Convenor

Atul Kumar Rai
Medical Social Worker
Poor Patient Assistance Cell, M.S. Office
PGIMER, Chandigarh-160012 (INDIA)
Email: atul.sw2007@gmail.com
Mobile No-09876656120

Message

Dear Friends

Welcome to the 5th Annual National Conference of AIAMSWP.

We are pleased to invite you to be a part of this historic experience to the 5th Annual National Conference of AIAMSWP. It is in this context and with this perspective that, the AIAMSWP has chosen the theme: **Social Work Intervention in Health/Mental Health Setup.**

As theme suggests, we wish to discuss and deliberate on issues and concerns emanating out of the contemporary persona and discourses of the profession.

We are confident that the conference shall certainly provide an excellent opportunity to all professionals, researchers, and practitioner to share their views, opinion and experiences on one platform.

We welcome you to GMCH &Chandigarh.

In Solidarity

Atul Kumar Rai

Chairperson Scientific Committee

Harbhajan Kaur
Social Activist

Residence
3608, Sector 46 C,
Chandigarh

Message

l send my best wishes for the 5th Annual National conference of All India Association of Medical Social Work Profession,. Conference which is being held in Government Medical College & Hospital, Sector 32, Chandigarh on dated 24th & 25th March 2018. The theme has been considerable awakening with regard to Social Work Intervention in Health/Mental Health Setup. For the success of this conference full co-operation is essential which lam glad to assure in an ample measure.

I wish the Conference great success.

Harbhajan Kaur 16/03/2018
Harbhajan Kaur

About the conference

The 5th Annual National Conference of All India Association of Medical Social Work Professionals (AIAMSWP) is in continuation of our previous four national conferences held at different Medical Institutions in India, jointly organised by AIAMSWP and Medical Social Work Professionals working in the various departments of respective institutes. The 1st, 2nd, 3rd and 4th seminars were held at PGIMER-Chandigarh, AIIMS-New Delhi, Safdarjung-New Delhi and KGMU, Lucknow, Uttar Pradesh respectively in the respective year from 2014 to 2017. This year the Medical Social Work Professionals of Government Medical College & Hospital, Chandigarh are organizing the 5th Annual National Conference. The purpose of this conference is to discuss and deliberate about the advancement of social work practice and research in health setup and other professional issues.

Theme: Social Work Intervention in Health/Mental Health Setup

Sub Themes

- Social Work Intervention for Prevention and Promotion of Health & Mental Health
- Hospital as a Family Unit and Medical Social Workers as Pillars
- Promoting Environmental Sustainability in Health Setup
- Social Work Intervention - Treatment and Rehabilitation
- Social Work Intervention in Hospital/ Medical Settings
- Social Work Practice in Promotion of Organ Donation
- Social Work Practice in the field of Mental Health
- Social Work Practice in the field of Maternity and Child Health
- Social Work Practice in the field of Disability
- Social Work Research in Health Care System
- Social Work Education, Action and Impact
- Social Work Practices in Public Health Issues - Creation of a Healthy Society
- Social Emergency Vs Clinical Emergency - Identification & Challenges
- Hospital as a Family Unit and Medical Social Workers as Pillars
- Corporate Social Responsibility in Prevention and Promotion of Health and Wellbeing

Organizers

Government Medical College & Hospital, Chandigarh was started for graduate i.e. MBBS and Postgraduate studies for the students belonging to Chandigarh in the year 1991 with the objectives of fulfilling the glaring deficiency of an undergraduate Medical College in the Union Territory of Chandigarh. At present, GMCH is under top ten Govt. Medical Colleges in India and running various medical and paramedical courses. For higher studies in the field of social work, M. Phil. in Psychiatric Social Work with 8 seats was started in 2013 under the Department of Psychiatry. Around 35 medical social work professionals are serving in various departments along with two faculties in the department of psychiatry.

All India Association of Medical Social Work Professionals

AIAMSWP was established AIAMSWP is a registered non-profit, non-political, national level organization dedicated to the promotion of standards and enhancement of the status of Social Work profession in health care in India.

AIAMSWP is one of first national level association of social work professionals working in health care in India. AIAMSWP was established in 2009 in the meeting in AIIMS New Delhi on 13 July 2009 and registered in 2011 under Society Act 1860 in Delhi, following the concerns of professional social workers to cater to the need of having an organization at the national level. Since its inception, it has been making attempts to bring professional social workers on one platform so that a collective identity of the profession could emerge. AIAMSWP intends to fulfil the twin purposes of promoting the social work profession in health care within the country together with safeguarding and protecting the interests of Social work professionals working in health care. Its Secretariat is located at PGIMER, Chandigarh and President's office is located at Safdarjung Hospital, New Delhi.

Aims and Objective:

i. To improve the standards of service, teaching, training and research on the subject of Medical and Psychiatric Social Work at all levels,

ii. To promote research in the specialty of Medical and Psychiatric Social Work, and the effective application of the knowledge acquired in teaching, training, research and services,

iii. To develop cooperation in teaching, training, research, and service between the departments of Medical and Psychiatric Social Work of various Medical Colleges/ Institutions in the country,

iv. To facilitate co-ordination amongst the departments of Medical and Psychiatric Social Work and other departments of Medical Colleges/ Institutions and Health Agencies/ Organizations,

v. To promote welfare of the professionals of Medical and Psychiatric Social Work, and

vi. To publish a journal which will be in furtherance of these aims, and will be the official organ of the Society.

Office Bearers of AIAMSWP

Patron	Dr. Anil K. Goswami	**Zonal Secretaries**		**Executive Members**
President	Ms. Rashmi Sharma	**North**	Sh. Raghavendra Kr. Rai	Sh. Subhasish Saha
Vice President	Sh. Ajay Kumar Singh Sh. Aftab Alam Shah	**Central**	Sh. Pankaj Singh	Sh. N. Singh
General Secretary	Dr. O. P. Giri	**East**	Sh. Narendra Kr. Singh	Sh Ashwani Singh
Joint Secretary	Sh. Sushil K. Mishra, Sh. B. R. Shekhar	**West**	Dr. Amar Vyas	Sh. Santosh Kr. Upadhyay
Treasurer	Mrs. Manpreet Kaur	**South**	Vacant	Sh. Anand Sharma
		North West	Sh. Shangam Rungsung	Sh. A. N. Singh

Medical Social Worker as a Member of Multi-Disciplinary Team

Hima Jacob Fernandez[1], Sooraj PS[2], Renjith R. Pillai[3*], Kamlesh Kumar Sahu[4]

[1]Mental Health Consultant, SN Educational Society, Kollam, Kerala

[2]Research Scholar, Department of Women's Studies, University of Calicut, Kerala

[3]Assistant Professor of Psychiatric Social Work, Dept. of Psychiatry, PGIMER, Chandigarh

[4]Associate Professor of Psychiatric Social Work, Dept. of Psychiatry, GMCH, Chandigarh

Abstract

Medical social work as a profession is becoming an integral element of a bio-psychosocial approach. The humanistic, empathetic and non-judgmental skills of a medical social worker improve the standards of treatment experiences of the patients. A medical social worker has training in social work, general/community medicine, psychology/psychiatry and sociology. This expertise makes him well skilled and equipped to play an indispensable role in a multidisciplinary team to provide holistic care for patients from all slants.

Keywords: medical social worker, multi-disciplinary team

Introduction

As the 20th century dawns, in the United States, hospitals took the lead role in providing effective care for the sick, gradually substituting home-based care. The locus of health care delivery system slowly moved towards the hospices. Tuberculosis, Sexually transmitted Diseases (STDs), Polio etc. were highly prevalent in the US those days. Dr. Richard C. Cabot, chief of medicine at Massachusetts General Hospital (MGH) realized that curative measures alone cannot effectively combat such issues. He came up with the proposal of appointing a Medical Social Worker at the hospital. In 1905, Garnet I. Pelton was appointed as the foremost medical social worker in the United States. Ida Cannon was the next to be appointed succeeding Mrs. Pelton in 1906. With the sincere efforts of the medical social workers, people were offered superior quality health care. Physicians remained confined to the treatment process, whereas the Medical social workers attended to their grievances and concerns, relieving and revitalising them. Dr. Ella Webb paved the way for Medical Social Workers in Ireland, as she launched a clinic for the children at the Adelaide Hospital, Dublin. Late in 1945, the Institute of Almoners, Britain was set in motion. Tata Institute of Social Sciences, Mumbai started incorporating Medical Social Workers in the team for health care delivery, starting on the history of Hospital Social Work in India. Slowly but steadily hospitals big and small, and medical colleges both in public and private sectors have started employing medical social workers.

Theoretical Background

People could be best understood in terms of their interaction with their individual environment. In other words, social environment plays a prominent role in determining the nature and prognosis of an illness. According to Cowles (2000), social environment refers to the quality and features of an individual's life conditions, taking into consideration their interpersonal relationships, resources for his or her requirements, the status and the roles he take part in the society. The reciprocal association of persons with their environment do not confine itself to medical social work even though. It is the core focus of Social Work practice as a whole. The concept of assessing people in terms of their social environment was named as the person-in-environment view and was set off by Dr. Cabot and Ida Cannon. The 'bio psycho social' approach in health care , have attained more and more prominence along with this. This approach is explicitly implemented by a Medical Social Workers. The 'bio psycho social approach' believes in the three inter-related aspects of the patient's environment:

1. The biological and therapeutic aspects of the health of the patient.
2. The psychological aspects like sense of self, self-esteem, and other emotional resources.
3. The social factors that encircle and have direct authority over the patient.

The Multidisciplinary Approach

Traditionally, the practice of medical social work has been characterized by uni-disciplinary thinking and individualistic. However, care of ill persons with complex and interactive health, social and functional needs is best achieved when the knowledge and skills of various health disciplines are shared and integrated. Multidisciplinary, collaborative health care practice is an effective means to plan, coordinate and implement care of a patient.

***Corresponding Author**:
Dr. Renjith R. Pillai,
Assistant Professor of Psychiatric Social Work,
Department of Psychiatry, PGIMER, Chandigarh.
Email: renjithpsw@gmail.com

Bartlett (1975) opined that the three central outcomes that a Medical Social Worker in a multidisciplinary team conveys are:

(1) Placing the patient and his or her individual needs as the axis of treatment;

(2) Acknowledging the fundamental idea of looking at the social phases of the disease in addition to providing high-quality patient service;

(3) Bringing in and highlighting the multidisciplinary approach in health care.

Including social workers in the process of health care brings many benefits not only to the clients, but to the other health professionals also. Medical Social workers acts as indispensable elements of the multidisciplinary team conveying effective utilization of time and resources and enhances work satisfaction in the fellow professionals. The multi-disciplinary team typically comprises a range of components, not necessarily belonging to a single institution, but with the common goal of delivering comprehensive care for the patients. Ideally, a team may include physicians, medical social workers, nurses, other professionals including occupational therapists, physiotherapists, recreational therapists, health instructors (eg: diabetes educator), surgeon, psychologist, psychiatrist, volunteer, support staff and family (as partners of care)

Medical Social Worker in a Multi Disciplinary Team

Medical social workers are the integral parts of a multi disciplinary health care team. They play a crucial role in hospital settings by helping patients and families in addressing the impact of the illness on the individuals and the family members. Tremendous stress often stems from the hospitalizations that are sudden and at times related to catastrophic nature of illness or injury. Stressors such as decreased personal control change in functional ability, information overload and reduced financial resources can lead to a range of emotional responses such as anger, anxiety and depression in family members.

Medical social workers as a part of the health care team provide assessment and appropriate interventions. They commonly provide individual, group and family intervention, crisis intervention at the time of crisis, patient/family education, resource mobilization, advocacy and referral services both in in-patient setting, out-patient setting and a community setting. They render psycho social care and other services to the patients and their families. Medical social workers often have specific expertise in the areas of Psychiatry, De-addiction, Neurology, Casualty and emergency set up, palliative care and community care.

Delivery of health services is a concept of working with a multidisciplinary team. The literature related to working with a multidisciplinary team in health services reveals a wide spread belief that collaboration among health care professionals is desirable and results in therapeutic benefits for client outcomes. Furthermore, it is perceived to enhance work satisfaction for health care professionals (Proctor-Childs, Feeman & Miller, 1998). Hospital social work in patient care offer the opportunity of working with other healthcare professionals such as Physician, Surgeon, Psychologist, Therapist, Nurse, Pathologist etc. The skills and knowledge of health professionals are needed to conduct a comprehensive multidimensional assessment of the physical, psychological, social, emotional, and functional status of an ill person. Medical social worker can effectively probe into almost all these areas of a patient.

Multidisciplinary team approach utilizes the skills and experience of individuals from health disciplines with each discipline approaching the patient from their own perspective. Most often, this approach involves separate individual consultations. This occurs in a "one-stop-shop" fashion with all consultations in a single day. Multidisciplinary team meets regularly in "case conference" to discuss about patient care in all aspects. Multidisciplinary team provides a medical social worker more knowledge and experience to work with patients. Medical social work in its very nature is multidisciplinary because of the many competencies required for promoting optimal levels of recovery from disabling disorders.

Each of the members in a multidisciplinary team performs exclusive and highly specific tasks though the services rendered by any member of the team cannot be substituted by the other. All of them contribute their services equally to restore the physical and social well being of the patient. The select services of a Medical Social Worker comprise the following;

Psychosocial Assessment (pre assessment)

With the aim to collect significant social information regarding the patient and to apply it in the process of evaluation, treatment and discharge planning phases, psychosocial assessment is carried out. The various forms of assessment that are undertaken by medical social workers is listed below:

- Initial Social Assessment: Social worker gathers information from the patient and the significant members and it moves through identifying current information, through historical patient and family data, to conclusions and recommendations for treatment and discharge planning.
- Interim Social Assessment: When a patient is re-admitted, informations are again re-collected to ascertain the changes since the last discharge.
- Annual Social Assessment: Long-stay patients are assessed annually and the changes are documented.
- Forensic Social Assessment: In cases involving legal interference, social worker works closely with physicians, psychiatrists and psychologists in preparing the evaluation report (MSHPP, 2007).

Psychosocial Intervention

The various modes of providing psychosocial interventions may be:

- Pre & post operative counseling
- Disability intervention
- Dealing with the requirements of the family members, pre-admission counseling
- Helping the patients to acquire essential documents.
- Psycho education and Income assessment
- Counseling for dealing with hospital anxiety and depression.
- Referrals for living provisions.
- Dealing with discharge issues and crisis intervention.

Post assessment

Aimed at assessing the necessary information regarding:

- The understanding of the disease and the treatment.
- The level of disability during discharge.
- The acquired and left out needs of the patient following the discharge.
- The burden the patient lays on the family members.
- The individual, familial and professional status of the patient after the discharge.

Documentation

It is important to record vital data pertinent to:

- Psychosocial assessment and intervention process
- The notes and issues discussed during multidisciplinary team consultant's rounds/reviews
- The discharge plan of the patient himself as well as the family members and the inputs made by the multi-disciplinary team.
- The level of progress in accomplishing the discharge plan made.

Specific roles

There are some specific roles to perform for a Medical Social Worker, which may include:

- Counseling the patient before admitting, so as to provide necessary information to him and to reduce the hospitalization anxiety.
- A detailed psychosocial evaluation of the patient done through case history taking.
- Clearing up the gaps in history taking and arriving at social diagnosis
- Interventions at individual, group and family level.
- Counseling before the discharge process.

(Muralidhar and Sinu, 2007)

Psycho-education

Critical details in the patient's diagnosis report are revealed and explained to the patient and the family members, skillfully. No details are hidden or unrevealed. 'Breaking the bad news' is often the task of a medical social worker. It is to be done with empathy, clarifying the causes for prognosis, the etiology as well as the prevalence rate.

Activity scheduling

It is important to utilize the time effectively for a person admitted in a hospital. Most of the patients fail in making use of their time effectively. Families as a result often complain that the ill person is 'lazy'. A medical social worker helps him or her by putting up a schedule of activities so that the time spent within the hospital is efficiently used by the patient. However, activity scheduling is subject to the level of disability of the patient.

Group intervention

Group interventions seeks for de-stressing the family members of patient, helping the patients in problem solving, assisting the patients to have a vivid understanding of their own problems and facilitating effective adaptation and rehabilitation.

Case management

Case management is carried out in a variety of ways including:

- Evaluation of specific psychosocial needs.
- Personal care plan.
- Linkage services and Referral.
- Observing the execution of the care plan, continually.
- Services of Advocacy.
- Observance of timely medication and foreseeable side-effects of it.
- Supportive Counseling.
- Follow up

Family intervention

Medical social workers specifically works with the family members and spends time with them for teaching them skills for tackling stress and widening their socialization .The process serves the purposes of dealing with the emotional issues of the families and patients for reducing relapse, burden, increasing the awareness and encouraging reasonable and practical expectations from the treatment process. (Muralidhar and Sinu, 2007).

Challenges Faced by Medical Social Worker in a Multi-disciplinary Team

- Professional conflicts, lack of respect or knowledge, lack of recognition and indifferent attitudes of fellow professionals.
- Supervision issues: lack of support from authorities and proper direction.
- Knowledge of **'how to work as part of a team'** is taken for granted only within the realm of professional training.
- Lack of clarity about the nature and functions of a Medical Social Worker
- Views of medical social workers not being considered in the admission, treatment and discharge procedures
- Issues related to convincing the patients and their care givers and the fellow workers with respect to the role of medical social workers.
- Weak knowledge base for working with a multidisciplinary team in healthcare
- Little researches evidences on effectiveness of medical social work interventions

Conclusion

Medical social work as a profession is slowly becoming an integral element of a bio-psychosocial approach. The profession comes into play with its humanistic, empathetic and non-judgmental skills to take on the allied treatment prerequisites and improves the standards of treatment experiences to the patients.

Besides patient care, medical social worker sensitizes the other associated professionals, about the need for empathy towards patients which in turn improves the quality of care. The assets of a medical social worker are his intensive training in social work, general/community medicine, psychology/psychiatry and sociology. He is well skilled and equipped in these above mentioned areas of specialties that are indispensable for a multidisciplinary team to provide holistic care for patients from all slants.

Reference

1. Bartlett, H. (1975). Ida M. Cannon: Pioneer in medical social work. *Social Service Review*, 49(2), 208–229.
2. Cowles, L. (2000). *Social work in the health field.* New York: Haworth Press.
3. Montana State Hospital Policy and Procedure (2007) Social Assessment. [Online] Available at URL. http://msh.mt.gov/volumeii/socialservices/socialassessment.pdf. [Accessed 12 January 2011].
4. Muralidhar D & Sinu E. (2007) Psychiatric Social Work Services in in-patient care settings. In: Sekar, K., Parthasarathy, K., Muralidhar, D., & Chandrasekar Rao, M. (eds.) *Handbook of Psychiatric Social Work.* 1st edition. Bangalore, NIMHANS Publications.
5. Proctor-Childs, Feeman & Miller (1998). Visions of teamwork: the realities of an interdisciplinary approach. *International Journal of Therapy and Rehabilitation.* 5(12): 616 – 635.

5th Annual National Conference of
All India Association of Medical Social Work Professionals

Scientific Programme

Time	Program	Resource Person/Presenter	Chairpersons
8.30 – 9.30 am	**Registration**		
09.30 -10.30am	**Inauguration**		
10:30-11.00 am High Tea			
11.00 am – 11.15 pm Keynote Address	Preamble to the Conference Themes "**Social Work Intervention in Health/Mental Health Setup**		Dr. C.P Singh
11.15 am –1.00pm Invited Lecturers: I (Hall A)	Technology and Health Issues: The Challenges for Professional Social Workers in Health Care Setting	Dr. D.P.Singh	Chairperson: Ms. Rashmi Sharma Dr. R.P Singh
	The Role of Corporate Social Responsibility in Prevention and Promotion of Health issues: Gimpses from Gujarat	Dr. Ankur Saxena	
	Mental Health Problems: Causes and Remedies	Dr. C.P Singh	
	Social Work intervention related to Health care	Dr. Monika Munjal	
	Family Intervention in Substance Abuse Treatment	Dr. Renjith R. Pillai	
1.00 pm - 2.00 pm Lunch			
2.00-3.00 pm Symposium (Hall A) Concurrent Session	Psycho-Social Rehabilitation in Mental Health: Pathway to Success	Narendra Kr. Singh, Bhupendra Singh, Parvesh Duhan, Prashant Srivastava	Chairperson: Dr. Ravi Jha Mr. Santosh K. Maurya
2.00-3.00 pm Oral Presentation: 1 (Hall B) Concurrent Session	Social Work Intervention in Promotion of Health	Ankur Saxena, Sneha Chandrapal	Chairperson: Dr. Asiya Nasreen Dr. Subhashish Saha
	Health Risk and Vulnerability of the People Working in the Marble Processing Units in Kishangarh, Ajmer district, Rajasthan	Rajeev M.M.	
	Corporate Social Responsibility and Women's Health Prevention and Promotion – A Study of CSR Initiatives of a Public Sector Undertaking	Ashvini Kumar Singh	
	Challenges among Social Workers in Hospital Settings: A Qualita tive Study on Role Confusion	Deepalatha R. Shetty, Krishan Kumar	
	Burden of Care and coping in care givers among People with Bipolar Affective Disorder	Menka, Neetu Sheokand, Rakesh Kumar, Pradeep Kumar	
	Social Work Intervention - Relocation and Rehabilitation of unattended/ unknown destitute patients in emergency in All India Institute of Medical Sciences Delhi	Leema, B.R.Shekhar, A.K.Chaurasiya, Abhishek, Aftab,Md. Shahid, Vivek	
2.00-3.00 pm Oral Presentation: 2 (Hall C) Concurrent Session	Organ procurement and transplantation: Social work interventions in Hospital Settings	Mukesh Kumar	Chairperson: Dr. Pradeep Kumar Mr. N. Singh
	Family of a Person with Severe Mental Illness: Intervention, Issues and Challenges	Saswati Chakraborti,	
	A Success Story of Heart Patient: Role of Medical Social Worker in Multi -professional Health Care Team	Sudha Gupta, Asha Rani	
	Adolescents in Orphanages: A Study of Academic Anxiety and School Adjustment	Hardeep Kaur, Arashmeet Chawla	
	Psychosocial Rehabilitation in Mental Health	Chandrabala	
	Transactional Analysis in Nursing as a Profession	Rohini Thapar, Navneet Nancy	
	Challenges for Social Work Education in India: Voices of Social Work Educator	Rajendra Baikady, Channaveer R.M, Cheng Shengl	
Poster Presentation (On the corridor, outside the Hall) 2.00-3.00Pm	Psychiatric Social Worker Services in Drug De -Addiction Centre	Neetu Rani	Chairperson: Dr. Hardeep Kaur Dr. Saswati Chakraborty
	Social Work Practice in the field of disability.	Komal Preet	
	Trauma care systems in India: An observational Study	Suruchi Sharma , Sushil K.Vimal, Sh.Ziley Singh Vical	
	Do male and female trauma patients receive the same pre hospital care? - An observationalfollow-up study in Delhi- NCR.	Suruchi Sharma	
	Mapping the knowledge and understanding of menstrual hygiene and menstrual health in Delhi rural and urban areas of Delhi.	Suruchi Sharma, Mohd. Yaseen, Sushil K.Vimal	
	Scope of Psychiatric Social Worker (PSW) in Community Mental Health Program: Field Experience and Observation	Krishan Kumar, Deepalatha R	
	Depression and Stress among Older Adults residing in Old Age Home	AvinashVerma, Prashant Srivastava	

Time	Program	Resource Person/Presenter	Chairpersons
3.00-4.00 pm Symposium - 1 (Hall A) Concurrent Session	Organ Donation and Transplantation: Challenges and Solutions	Dr. Vipin Koushal, Mrs.Saryu, Ms.Neelakshi	Chaiperson: . Prof. S.K Arya Dr. Renjith R. Pillai
3.00-4.00 pm Oral Presentation: (Hall B) Concurrent Session	Caregivers Challenges of Hospitalized Elderly	Ushvinder Kaur Popli, Rishi Panday	Chaiperson: Dr. Rajeev M.M. Mr. Prashant Srivastav
	Brief Intervention with caregivers of people living with schizophrenia	Bhupendra Singh, Priti Singh	
	Role of Medical Social Worker in Neuro psychiatric hospital	Pappu Rajak	
	Cancer Patients in Punjab:An Overview	Talwinder Kaur	
	Effect of Emotional Maturity on Mental Health	Ruchi Chauhan	
	Depression, Anxiety and Stress among Alcohol Dependence patients	Reena, Sunila, Bhupendra Singh	
	Gender difference in family attitude and Family burden people living with schizophrenia	Monika, Bhupendra Singh	
	Social Work Intervention in Disability: A study	Khillare Dinesh Digambar	
3.00-4.00 pm Award Category Presentation –1 (Hall C) Concurrent Session	Patient Satisfaction Regarding Quality of Hospital Services in Cardiology Outpatient Department in a Tertiary Care Government Hospital, South India	Ramaraju Jayalakshmi, Subitha Lakshminarayanan Santhosh Satheesh	Chairperson: Mr. B.R Shekhar Mr. Pankaj Singh
	Resilience and vulnerability in Parents of Child with Intellectual Disability (ID)	Krishan Kumar and Deepalatha R	
	Application of Motivational Enhancement Therapy in Group settings among Patients with Substance Abuse	Kuldeep Singh, Prashant Srivastava, Savita Chahal	
	Impact of non-pharmacological aspects in the community based treatment of substance Abuse in a Resettlement Colony, Sunder Nagari, Delhi	Ratnesh Kumar	
	Quality of life among female elderly living in old age home and community	Rishi Panday Pradeep Kumar	
	Assessment of the scope for social work intervention for the effective Utilization of Janani Shishu Suraksha Karyakram (JSSK): KAP study amongst Post-natal women in Sub Centre Dighi- Jikthan, District Aurangabad	Rosy Joseph Sanjay Bhonge, Rajaram Gavade, Kalpna Pandit& Deepak Raut	

Day 2

Time	Program	Resource Person/Presenter	Chairpersons
8.00-09.30 Am Invited Lectures-II (Hall A) Concurrent Session	Social Work Practice in Indian Scenario: A Health Perspective	Dr. Ashvini Kumar Singh	Chairperson: Dr. Anuradha Mrs. Sudha Gupta
	Institutionalization to De-Institutionalization to Residential Care Setting: Changing Scenario	Dr. Pravin B. Yannawar	
	Human Rights of Person Living with Mental Illness	Dr. Bhupendra Singh	
8.00-09.30 Am Award Category Presentation – 2 (Hall B) Concurrent Session	Severity of violence and quality of life of women with psychiatric illness as compared to normal controls	Sapna Kumari,Manisha Kiran,S Choudhary	Chairperson: Dr. Kamlesh Kr. Sahu Dr. Anil K. Goswami
	Knowledge and awareness regarding fertility and reproductive factors, their as sociation with socio economic status among Indian Women	Shobha Kandpal, Dr Monika Gupta, Dr Reeta Mahey, Dr P. Vanamail, Dr Neena Malhotra, Dr Neeta Singh, Dr Alka Kriplani.	
		.	
	The Role of Mental Health Intervention in Gender Affirmative Therapy	Srabasti Majumdar	
	Impact of coping styles and resources & academic aspirations on the psychological well -being in school going adolescents	Neha Roy, D.Ram, Vani Narula, Dipanjan Bhattacharjee	
	Understanding the recovery process of male youth from alcohol abuse in the rehabilitation centres in Guwahati, Assam	Nabanita Hazarika	
	Social Work practices in Public Health issues - Creation of a healthy society	Komal Preet	
8.00-09.30 Am Award Category Presentation – 3 (Hall C) Concurrent Session	Children with Type 1 Diabetes: A holistic approach of Professional Social Work Practice towards its Management	Jyoti Kakkar, Srishti Puri	Chairperson: Dr. O.P Giri Mr. Santosh Upadhyay
	Effects of strength based supportive therapy on family functioning and coping among persons with alcohol dependence syndrome	Shrikant Pawar,Niteen Abhivant, Praful Kapse, Manisha Kiran, Amool R Singh	
	Prevalence and Psycho-Social Determinants of Deliberate Self Harm in Students	Avadhesh Kumar, Manushi Srivastava	
	Globalization and Promotion of Tobacco Product at Point of Purchase: A Public Health Issue:	Viney dhiman	
	Psychosocial Function and Mental Health among Medical Students	Neetu Sheokand, Pradeep Kumar	
	Social Work Intervention for Prevention and Promotion of Mental Health in Vitiligo patients - A study	Dhirendra Patel	
	Assessment of Knowledge attitude and practices regarding HIV/AIDS and role of social work/counseling interventions amongst the ANC mothers attending the ICTC at Tanda Medical College	AnamikaChanchal, Sanjay Bhonge, Desh Raj, Ankush Kaushal, Rajaram Gavade, Dinesh Kumar and Deepak Raut	
9.30-10.30 Am Workshop (Hall A)	Living Life Positively	Gurvinder Pal Siingh, Mr. Jasvir Singh, Dr. Rajnish	Dr. Seema Vinayak
10:30 -11.00 High Tea			
11:00- 12.30 AM Symposium – 3 (Hall A) Concurrent Session	Challenges and Concerns in Psychiatric Social Work Practice:A Current Perspective	Rishi Pandey,Kuldeep Singh, Prashant Srivastav	Chairperson: Dr. Kalindi N. Ranbhara Mr. Narendra K. Singh

Time	Program	Resource Person/Presenter	Chairpersons
11.00-12.30 **Oral Presentation – 4** **(Hall B)** **Concurrent Session**	Challenge Resolutions among Social Workers in Hospital Settings: A Qualitative Study	Deepalatha R. Shetty	Chairperson: Dr. Rajnish Mr. Bhonge S. Sadanand
	The roles and responsibilities of psychiatric social work for promotional aspects of mental health	Urvashi	
	Rashtriya Swasthya Bima Yojana (RSBY): Policy Planning and Implementation: A Comparison between Kerala and Madhya Pradesh State)	Usman	
	Life Satisfaction among the spouses of individuals with alcohol dependence syndrome as compared with normal control	Mayank Singh, Jai Shanker Patel, Manisha Kiran	
	Social worker intervention in surgical Gastroenterology patients	R.Srividhya, Biju Pottakkat, V. Chitraleka	
	Sex education of children and adolescents with mental illness	Nandini Sharma	
	Social Work Practic es in Promotion of Organ Donation	Isha Goswami	
11.00-12.30 **Scientific Oral Presentation** **(Hall C)** **Concurrent Session**	To study the Burnout in health care professionals working in Govt. & Private Instuitions.	Kaplu Sharma, Atul Kumar Rai	Chairperson: Mr. Atul Kumar Rai Mr. Suresh Pal
	Organ Donation: A Qualitative Study Exploring the Reasons Behind Living Organ Donation	Nishtha Mishra, MuthusamySivakami	
	Level of Awareness about blood donation in Rural & Urban Community: A Comparative Study	Pardeep Kumar, Atul Kumar Rai	
	Marriage: Role and Contribution in Mental Illness	Divya Rai	
	Social work practice in open defecation free movement: A special reference to rural District of North India	Ravindra Khaiwal, Sanjeev Kumar	
	Socio-demographics and Social Participation of Disabled Women: An Exploration based upon Rehabilitation Centres of West Tripura	Subhasish Saha, Durba Deb, Haimanti Sarkar	
	Mindfulness based cognitive therapy for depression and generalized anxiety disorder: A comparative study	Sweta, Upendra Singh	
	Breastfeeding and Health outcomes for Infant: A study conducted in slum area of Lucknow city	Vijai Sharma	
	Corporate Social Responsibility- An instrument for promoting supportable healthcare practices	Rifat Anjum	
12.30-1.30PM **Oral Presentation – 5** **(Hall A)** **Concurrent Session**	**Professional Social Worker's Voice towards Overcoming Challenges in Hospital Settings: A Qualitative Study**	Deepalatha R. Shetty , Krishan Kumar	Chairperson: Dr. Soma Sahu Mr. Sushil K. Mishra Ms. Manpreet
	Comparison of life events in individuals with Bipolar Affective Disorder and Healthy Control	Jai Shanker Patel , Manisha Kiran	
	Community Based Rehabilitation and Person with Disability: An Emerging Issue in India	Neetu, Meneka, Rakesh Kumar & Pradeep Kumar	
	Behaviour Problems in Children and Adolescents with Intellectual Disability and Functional Psychosis	Jagritee Singh, N. K. Singh	
	Level of Determination and Dependence among person with Alcohol Dependence	Rakesh Kumar , Neetu Sheokand & Pradeep Kumar	
	Social Worker in Hospital: A bridge between patient and administration for smooth functioning of services in hospital.	S.K Srivastava	
	Role Perception and Role Performance of Professional Social Workers in Hospital Settings	Shashi Kant Srivastava, Bijendra Pradhan	
12.30-1.30PM **Oral Presentation – 6**	Stress and care giving burden among parents having children with autism	Jyoti Kakkar, Prashant Srivastava	Chairperson: Dr. Jaswinder Kaur Ms. R. Jayalaxmi
	Challenges for Social Work Education in India: Voices of Social Work Student	Rajendra Baikady Channaveer R.M,Cheng Shengl	

Welcome Delegates

Technology and Health Issues: The Challenges for Professional Social Workers in Health Care Settings

Dr. D P Singh

Professor and Head, Department of Social Work, Punjabi University, Patiala, Email: mordps@gmail.com

The impact of technology has extended into the realm of health care. The development of new technologies has incredibly changed the way of treatment in health care organizations and the interaction with the patients. Use of medical devices and communication technology in monitoring disease and symptoms is a commonplace in health care institutions. The innovations in technology have helped health care executives moved towards new ways like the electronic health records, barcoding, radio frequency identification, telemedicine and tele-health. With the technological boom, there is no doubt that there is a paradigm shift in all areas of health care; nevertheless, in a number of observable areas, the development of technology has affected health care in negative ways as well. The researches in health care have observed that there is link between certain mental illnesses and the use of internet and social media. The internet and internet-based platforms including smart phone applications tend to make people less happy, lonely and reduces self-esteem. Individuals having internet addiction are far likely to experience mental health problems than those who use it moderately.

Against this backdrop, present paper underscores that while technology has great ability to transform the health care industry, it has negative sides too. Technology adversely affects our mental and physical well-being in a significant way. Technology has decreased our ability to empathize and increased social freezing. Technology has impacted our relationships and ability to create and sustain intimacy. Altogether new challenges have emerged for health care executives particularly the professional social workers in health care settings. Thus in order to promote wellness and healthy living, we need to tread cautiously while using new technologies.

Keywords: Technology, Health, Professional Social Workers

Mental Health Problems in India: An Urgent Call to the Profession

Dr. Daya Singh Sandhu

Senior Fulbright-Nehru Research Scholar, Punjabi University Patiala, Lindsey Wilson College, USA
Email: dayasandhu29@hotmail.com

As part of the rapid economic and social changes in India, people are experiencing significant multiple stressors in their lives. Some of these stressors are causing some very serious mental health concerns including, clinical depression, anxiety, mental distress, marital discords, domestic violence, and serious alcoholism and substance abuse problems. I identified six major categories of mental health problems in India at this time which included: Psychosomatic disorders; drugs and alcohol abuse; domestic violence; inter-generational conflicts; mood disorders and mood swings; superstitions problems relating to black magic, supernatural forces, and witchcraft. If suicide is an ultimate indicator of psychological distress and psychopathology, it sends a stunning warning that something is seriously wrong with the psychological health of India. In 2017 alone, 1,35000 persons committed suicide in India. At least ten times more Indian students and farmers have suicide ideations. Unfortunately, the rate of suicides keeps on escalating and there seems to be no end in sight. In addition to other mental health issues, this presentation will specifically focus on the strategies to curb the rate of suicides and suicide ideations.

Keywords: Mental Health, India

Institutionalization to De-Institutionalization to Residential Care Setting: Changing Scenario

Dr. Pravin B. Yannawar[1], Dr. Jahanara M. Gajendragad[2]

[1]Associate Professor, [2]Senior Psychiatric Social Worker,
Dept. of Psychiatric Social Work, Institute of Human Behaviour and Allied Sciences, Delhi
Email: pravin007yann@gmail.com

In the last two decade the Indian society has seen drastic changes in the field of mental health. Awareness about the mental illness has increased multifold, so as the need to seek the treatment and its exodus. Most of the psychiatric hospitals are now in the main stream of the health service delivery system.

De-institutionalisation is the process of replacing long-stay psychiatric hospitals with less isolated community mental health services for those diagnosed with a mental disorder or developmental disability. In the late 20th century, it led to the closure of many psychiatric hospitals, as patients were increasingly cared for at home or in halfway houses, clinics and regular hospitals. In the early sixties we have seen the Institutionalized care for the persons with mental illness, where there was popular believe "Once a mentally ill, is always mentally Ill", but now gone those days. Now people realize that, most of the mental illnesses are treatable, society has come long way from Institutionalization to De-Institutionalisation. People are not only ready to accept people with mental illnesses, but also working towards their reintegration within the family and also back into the main stream society.

However very few percentage of the person required the Institutionalised or long term care because of their very nature of the illness, society at large may not be in the position to accept them, but they can be better placed and rehabilitated in the residential care setting. Many countries have moved further from "deinstitutionalization" to "re-institutionalisation", or relocation to different institutions, has begun, as evidenced by increases in the number of supported housing facilities, forensic psychiatric beds, and the growing prison population.

The emergence of concept of Half Way Home or Long Stay Home for this kind of clientele has been considered as very progressive mode, and good development. In these days many private organization have setup HWH/LSH in metropolitan cities and giving their best in taking care of these clienteles and engaging them in the therapeutic activities. Many Government Institutions like IHBAS in Delhi has started its own HWH/LSH and providing the much needed help to the families of person with long term mental illness.

Keywords: De-Institutionalisation, Residential Care, Half Way Home

Social Work Intervention in Health Care Setting

Dr. Monica Munjial Singh

Centre for Social Work, Panjab University, Chandigarh. Email - mona13mch@pu.ac.in

The role a social worker can play in a health field is to work towards the enhancement of a person's social and emotional functioning which can be achieved through targeted interventions and the mobilisation of services and supports. Intervention is done by the Social Worker's after the recognition of the impact which socio-economic, cultural, psychological and political determinants have on the health and overall well-being of a person's relationships and social environments. The focus is on the holistic care at the health setting with the capability to consider the complexities involving psychosocial, ethical and legal issues where in the social workers offer a valuable and exclusive contribution by providing appropriate services in order to meet the multidimensional needs at the primary method levels working with individuals, families and groups. Professional social workers are present throughout the health field across a wide range of settings which include Hospitals, PHC's, Mental Health Settings, Government, Charitable Health Care Institutions, Policy Programmes related to Health, De-addiction services etc. to name a few. In order to sort out the complex issues such as social, psychological, family and institutional dynamics which impact a person's health social workers are regularly involved. A Social worker ensures that within the health care system the individuals are able to make the right decisions which concerns their health and well being and all the information is accessible to them. In the health care setting the scope of practice is drawn on varied theories, skills, techniques and expertise in order to reach out to the client's situation by understanding it in a comprehensive manner and analysing it in totality. Social diagnosis identifies the problems and need based interventions address the social and emotional issues which are impacting the individual in totality. Social Work intervention in a health care setting is based on a multifaceted approach in which each and every aspect is very important and inter-dependent.

Keyword: Social Work, Intervention, Health

Family Intervention in Substance Abuse Treatment

Dr. Renjith R. Pillai

Assistant Professor of Psychiatric Social Work, PGIMER, Chandigarh
Email: renjithpsw@gmail.com

All over the World and in India, substance misuse is a common occurrence. Licit and illicit substance uses are a concern in the public health. According to National Mental Health Survey (2017), alcohol and tobacco are the most commonly abused substances followed by Cannabis. In Punjab, 1-40% population use opioids, cannabis, sedatives (especially benzodiazepines) and inhalants. Family bear the brunt of substance abuse among its members. The family environmentcan maintainthe substance use behaviours or cause relapse. Psychosocial interventions especially focusing the family issues in addition to the medical management is the responsibility of the psychiatric social workers in the multi-disciplinary team. Psychiatric Social Workers, undertake comprehensive assessment of the family dynamics, makes conclusions, intervene and create research evidences.

Keywords: Family, Substance abuse, Intervention

The Role of Corporate Social Responsibility in Prevention and Promotion of Health Issues: Glimpses from Gujrat

Prof. Ankur Saxena

Dept. of Social Work, The Maharaja Sayajirao University Baroda
Email: saxena_ankur2@gmail.com

The significance of Corporate Social Responsibility is increasing day by day not only nationally but globally. Recently held Annual World Economic Forum at DAVOS 2018 was a great platform for corporates around the world to depict their views on Corporate Responsibility. Much is spent on curative aspect of health and not on the preventive aspect. The government spending is less on health and health has to be considered as a social determinant.

The paper aims to explore CSR practices particularly in the context of prevention and promotion health issues in the rural as well as urban sector. The question arises "Do the Corporates consider health as an issue to be taken care of?" If so, what are the initiatives taken up as a part of their business strategy and the paper will showcase some glimpses on the role of CSR in prevention and promotion of health issues in Gujarat.

1.

Psycho-Social Rehabilitation in Mental Health: Pathway to Success

Narendra Kumar Singh[1], Bhupendra Singh[2], Parvesh Duhan[3], Prashant Srivastava[4]

[1]Psychiatric Social Worker, Central Institute of Psychiatry, Ranchi, Jharkhand
[2]Assistant Professor, Dept. of Psychiatric Social Work, Institute of Mental Health, Rohtak, Haryana.
[3]Research Scholar , Punjab University, Chandigarh
[4]Psychiatric Social Worker, Kalpana Chawla Govt. Medical College and Hospital, Karnal, Haryana.

India has some 40 to 80 million persons with mental disability. But low literacy, few jobs and widespread social stigma are making mentally ill people among the most excluded in India. Person with mental illness are less likely to be in esteemed positions, mentally disabled adults are more likely to be unemployed, and families of mental ill members are often worse off than average. Psycho-social rehabilitation aims to reduce stigma and handicap and promote equity and opportunity, its proponents engage in organizational, legislative, professional, quality of care and quality of life assurance, family organization and support, self help and participation, educational and promotive efforts to strengthen services, expansion of services and research, and improvement of delivery systems. As such, PSR aims at helping individuals to fully enjoy all their rights, as expressed in international legal instruments and, when appropriate, by national laws.

Keywords: Psycho-Social Rehabilitation, Mental Health, Concerns and Challenges

Sub Theme of the Facilitator

[1]Psycho-Social Rehabilitation in Hospital Settings

[2]Community Based Psycho-Social Rehabilitation

[3]Cognitive Rehabilitation in Mental Health

[4]Concerns and Challenges in Psycho-Social Rehabilitation

2.

Organ Donation and Transplantation: Challenges and Solutions

Vipin Koushal[1], Saryu[2], Neelakshi[3]
[1]Additional Professor Dept. of Hospital Administration & Nodal Officer ROTTTO
[2]Consultant IEC, ROTTO, PGIMER Chandigarh
[3]Transplant Coordinator, ROTTO, PGIMER Chandigarh.

Life is a dynamic process. It starts from birth and ends into death. In between, human beings have to experience many changes, transitions, upheavals and impediments in life. Organ transplantation has been emerged as an emerging field of modern medical discipline i.e. regenerative medicine. In India organ transplantation and donation has not been able to get the attention of common people as well as clinical professionals. But in this country the issue of organ donation has to be given paramount importance to cater the increased need of people. A large section of the common people and even trained clinicians do possess very limited and faulty ideas and notions about organ donation. Comprehensive measures can be taken by government to improve their conditions since satisfied workers are more motivated, productive and fulfilled. They can also contribute to awareness in organ donation

Keywords: Organ Donation, knowledge, professionals

Sub Theme of the Facilitator

[1]Legal and ethical aspects of Organ donation and Transplantation

[2]Awareness strategy and plan in Organ Donation programme.

[3]Psychosocial issues and challenges in Organ Transplant Programme

3.

Challenges and Concerns in Psychiatric Social Work Practice: A Current Perspective

Rishi Panday[1], Kuldeep Singh[2], Prashant Srivastava[3]

[1]Psychiatric Social Worker, Half Way Home, Dept. of Social Welfare, Govt. of NCT of Delhi, New Delhi
[2,3]Psychiatric Social Worker, Kalpana Chawla Govt. Medical College and Hospital, Karnal, Haryana

There is an increasing trend toward greater inclusion of inter professional collaborative care models in the health care system. Collaborative models bring various health care providers together such as physicians, psychiatrist, nurses, psychiatric/medical social workers, psychologists, pharmacists, dietitians, and others to provide team-based care. Key factors can help influence or deter successful collaboration. Social work has historical experience in team based care and brings a unique perspective to health care environments. The psychiatric social worker provides individual, family, and group social work counseling and other social work treatment interventions to psychiatric hospital patients, in community and assumes primary responsibility for discharge planning. Psychiatric social work practice is both challenging and rewarding. Heavy caseloads, struggling clients, less recognitions and impoverished neighborhoods are examples of the problems facing psychiatric social workers today.

Keywords: Concerns, Challenges, Psychiatric Social Work

Sub Theme of the Facilitator

[1]Psychiatric Social Work Practice: An Overview

[2]Challenges in Psychiatric Social Work Practice

[3]Concerns and Future Steps in Psychiatric Social Work Practice

Prevalence and Psycho-Social Determinants of Deliberate Self Harm in Students

Avadhesh Kumar[1], Manushi Srivastava[2]

[1]Research Scholar [2]Assistant Professor & Supervisor
Dept. of Community Medicine, Institute of Medical Sciences (IMS), BHU, Varanasi.
Email: avadhbhu@gmail.com

Background: Deliberate Self-Harm (DSH) is a challenging public health issue which is single most important risk factor for suicide. Deliberate self-harm (DSH) is common among young people is usually precipitated by stressful life problems; however, there is scanty data on this issue from India. Objectives: Therefore this study is planned to find the incidence of DSH and to study the associated psycho-social and demographic factors among students who involved in the act of harming themselves. Material and methods: This cross sectional study was conducted within 340 students at the student health centre of Banaras Hindu University Varanasi, Uttar Pradesh, India. Data collected by semi-structured interview schedule which documented the socio-demographic variables, psycho-social factors, family history and the details about the act of DSH. Results: The prevalence of DSH in this study sample was 18.2%, which was significantly associated (p = 0.015) with gender. Past history of self harm, history of Psychiatric Disorder, Habit of substance abuse and physical abuse also showed significant association with gender. However family history of suicide had no association with gender (0.526). Family quarrel (25.8%) and problem in love relationship (17.7%) were found to be the most common precipitating reasons for DSH. Conclusion: Socio-demographic and clinical variables such as peer group adjustment, environment in neighborhood, relation with other siblings and parenting style should be probed. This type of research is alarming call for health care professionals for early identification of the problem so that necessary intervention can be done at an early stage.

Keywords: Self-Harm, Student, Abuse, Psycho-social, Family history.

Assessment of Knowledge Attitude and Practices regarding HIV/AIDS and Role of Social Work/Counseling Interventions amongst the ANC Mothers attending the ICTC at Tanda Medical College

AnamikaChanchal[1], Sanjay Bhonge[2], Desh Raj[3], AnkushKaushal[4], RajaramGavade[5], Dinesh Kumar[6], Deepak Raut[7]

[1]Health Educator, Tanda Medical Collage Tanda,
[2]Social Worker, FWTRC Mumbai,
[3]MD Community medicine, Medical College Chamba,
[4]MSW Dept. of Community Medicine, Tanda Medical College,
[5]Statistical Assistant, FWTRC, Mumbai,
[6]Associate Professor, Dept. of Community Medicine, Medical College, Tanda,
[7]Director FWTRC Mumbai. Email: anamikachanchal7@gmail.com

Introduction: HIV counseling and testing service is a key entry point to prevention of HIV infection and to treatment and care of people who are infected with HIV. Objective of the study: The study aims to understand the KAP amongst the ANC mothers attending the ICTC center and identify the role of social work/counseling intervention and to determining the association between source of HIV information and HIV knowledge, Misconception about the mode of transmission, attitude towards PLWHA and practices about the condom use. Method and Material: The data was collected from 181 ANC mothers with Purposive sampling method and after prior consent at OBG-OPD at Tanda Medical College during August 2017 to September 2017. A semi structured survey questionnaire was administered as a face-to-face personal interview, and participant answers were filled in by interviewer's Analyses were performed using Excel and SPSS software. Descriptive statistics were used to describe demographics and sources of HIV/STD information. Results: The demographic distribution the study participants show that 146(80.7%) participants were from the age group of 31-40. Out of 181 most of the participants 82 (45.3%) participants were educated up to intermediate level and 51(28.2%) were graduation & above. Majority of were mostly house wife 166(91.7%). Only 41(22.7%) women family income was in range of 5000 per month and 34(18.8%) were having family income more than 20000. The cast distribution shows that 80(44.2%) women belong to other backward class. Pregnant women 171(94.5%) have heard about the HIV/AIDS before visiting the ICTC. 132(72.9%) women was aware that the use of condom can prevent transmission of HIV/AIDS and 153(84.5%) said that it can be prevented by remaining faithful with single partner. According to study data 106(58.6%) mothers know all the correct modes of HIV transmission, 27(14.9%) mothers know three modes of transmission i.e. unprotected sex, unsafe/infected blood products and infected needles. 20 (11.1%) don't know any mode of transmission, whereas 5 (2.8%) mothers know unprotected sex and infected mother to child transmission. The table about the misconception revealed that 38.7 % participants believe that through mosquito bite they can be affected. While 19.9 still believe that sharing a toilet can infect them. Wearing cloths of infected person, eating and drinking in same plate or shaking hands can transmit infection are some other misconception still prevailing in amongst women. Recommendation: The study highlights that the social work/counseling interventions need to be strengthened and made more gender sensitive. The ICTC have male counselor hence due to gender issues the ANC mothers may be having communication gap. So there is need for trained female social worker/counselor at the facility to counsel the mothers attending the clinic which can help the mother to interact with the counselors more easily.

Keywords: HIV/AIDS, ICTC, Counseling, Social Work, ANC

Social Work Intervention for Prevention and Promotion of Mental Health in Vitiligo Patients – A Study

Dhirendra Patel

Research Scholar, Department of Social Work, Gujarat University, Ahmadabad
Email: dhirendra1972@gmail.com

As per The World Health Organization (WHO) defined human health in its broader sense in its 1948 constitution as "a state of complete physical, mental, and social well-being and not merely the absence of disease or infirmity. So, Physical, Mental and Social Well-being are the 3 key aspect for human health. Physical health is handle by medical practitioners while mental and social well-being be taken care by social worker. In the past few decades we are noticing significant developments in our understanding of mental health. With that,The role of social worker for Mental and Social Well-being of Individual is also changing and increasing it's importance too. With the Patients of Vitiligo also, their physical conditions be taken care by doctors but for their mental and social wellbeing needs to be taken care by social worker with intervention for prevention and promotion of their mental health. The condition of people with Vitiligo is still same and not changing much more. Vitiligo is a skin decease which convert the normal brown skin in to white skin. Around the globe, from 1% to 8% of population is suffering from Vitiligo. Focal, Segmental, Acro-Facial, Vulgaris and Universalis are different type of vitiligo. Vitiligo is having direct impact on Quality of Life of patients. Vitiligo patients are many time facing discrimination and humiliation due to their skin problem. Even sometimes they feel stigma and human right violations by community people intentionally or unintentionally. Vitiligo impact on their daily life is so serious sometime, it leads towards isolation, depression and many times towards suicidal Tendency or towards suicide. Vitiligo is having impact on Psychological Conditions, Interpersonal Relations, Family Relations and Social Life. Social Work Intervention for Prevention and Promotion of Mental Health in Vitiligo Patients is the purpose of this paper.

Keyword: Social Work Intervention, Prevention and Promotion of Mental Health, Vitiligo

Children with Type 1 Diabetes: A holistic approach of Professional Social Work Practice towards its Management

Jyoti Kakkar[1], Srishti Puri[2]

[1]Professor, [2]Ph.D Scholar Dept. of Social Work, Jamia Millia Islamia, New Delhi
Email: puri.s1990@gmail.com

The paper is based on empirical data from 50 families who have children suffering from Type 1 diabetes. Different aspects of socio-psychological response to the ailment are seen. Type 1 diabetes is occurring in children at a very early age and its incidence is increasing in India. The diagnosis, impact upon the child's schooling, peer relationships, sibling relationship, etc are quite serious and affect the families in many ways. Also the parents' of these children face immense stress and sometimes depression. For some of them it may mean giving up their careers or making adjustments. Social interactions and family interactions are no more the same. In fact some refrain from even sharing the health status of the child with friends and relatives. It is a study based on mixed method approach. The findings have been discussed and also the nature of interventions that have been used by the professional social worker. Parents coping mechanism of this chronic ailment of their child has been studied. An approach of having a social worker working along with a pediatrics endocrinologist has been found to be effective. Also role of a social worker in mobilizing resources such as blood glucose testing facilities, diagnostic tests, educating the child on proper diet and exercise, and referral to specialists if required have been described. Also the use of technology to bring parents together on a common platform has been initiated and found workable.

Keywords: Type 1 diabetes, chronic illness, social work intervention

Social Work practices in Public Health issues - Creation of a healthy society

Komal Preet

BDS Intern, Adesh University, Bathinda, Punjab Email: komalpreet386@gmail.com

Social workers play a huge role in Public Heath. Public Health Social Workers focus on prevention and identity children, adults, families and communities with needs. And provide intervention services to help these people discover ways of meeting their needs and preventing future problems. One of the ways Public Health Social workers do this involves helping individuals and families make Behavioral and situational life changes in order to improve their overall health and well-being. Their focus extends to communities as well and a major part of that is addressing broad public health issues. Their works provide a comprehensive understanding of health issues from a social- cultural perspective. Social workers are instrumental in building the bridge between communities and government agencies working in this direction. The major characteristic of Public Health Social Work is an epidemiological approach to identifying social problems affecting the health status and social functioning of all population groups with an emphasis on intervention at primary prevention level.

Keywords: Social Work, public Health, Creation Society

Application of Motivational Enhancement Therapy in Group settings among Patients with Substance Abuse

Kuldeep Singh[1], Prashant Srivastava[1]

[1]Consultant, Psychiatric Social Worker,
Dept. of Psychiatry, Kalpana Chawla Government Medical College and Hospital, Karnal, Haryana,
Email: kuldeep.olla@gmail.com

Background: Substance abuse is defined as use of a drug or any other substance for a non-medical purpose with the aim of producing some type of "mind altering "effect in the users. This includes both the legal and illegal drugs. Psychoactive substance use poses a threat to the health, social and economic fabric of families, communities and nations. Group Therapy is most common non-pharmacological interventions used to treat alcohol dependence. It is economical and allows one health care professional to conduct the session. Group therapy affords patients the opportunity to hear from others dealing with the same issue, and acceptance received from peers in group therapy can help combat the social stigma associated with alcohol dependence. Aims and Objectives: Present study aims to assess and compare desire to quit substance use among substance users and effectiveness of Motivation Enhancement Therapy on desire to quit substance use in experimental group. Sample and Sampling: A total number of n=60 participants were selected using purposive sampling technique. Sample comprised of 30 patients inpatient unit and 30 from the out-patient department of psychiatry, Kalpana Chawla Government Medical College and Hospital, Karnal as per inclusion and exclusion criteria. Results and Conclusions: Results and Conclusions will be discussed during time of presentation.

Keywords: Motivation Enhancement Therapy, Group and Substance Abuse

Resilience and Vulnerability in Parents of Child with Intellectual Disability

Krishan Kumar[1], Deepalatha R[1]

[1]PhD. Scholar TISS Mumbai, Email: krishan2056@gmail.com

Intellectual disability (ID) can found around the world, an estimation of 2 to 3% of population suffer with ID. Person with ID face difficulty in physical activities, social learning, motor activities in day to day life. This is not limited to individual problem but also brings several other problems and affects to person with ID as well as people attached to him/her. Parents are intimate care giver to any child; therefore children with ID are also their responsibility. Parents face multiple difficulties in physical care, financial arrangement for treatment, social exclusion, social stigma etc. These difficulties expose them to several psychosomatic issues. So, while dealing with these psycho-social issues, we must need to understand parent's difficulties. Present study aims to lighten the positive and negative impacts on parents. This study targets parents of children with ID, studying in special schools in Puducherry (UT). With help of structured tool, Mothers and fathers both were interviewed. Mothers face more difficulties' compare to fathers and they found with high positive as well as negative impact. Mothers make high career adjustment and face loss of social support because of having child ID. Mothers observed with high resilience compare to male counter parts. In end part study also discuss regarding scope of intervention by Professional Social Work (PSWs) to deal with their issues.

Keywords: Intellectual Disability, Psychosocial impact, Parents and Resilience

Understanding the Recovery Process of Male Youth from Alcohol Abuse in the Rehabilitation Centres in Guwahati, Assam

Nabanita Hazarika

Research Scholar, Tata Institute of Social Sciences, Guwahati,
Email: nabanita.hazarika2016@tiss.edu

The study is carried out in the rehabilitation centres of Guwahati, Assam, to understand the youth who are recovering from alcohol abuse. The study highlights the risk and protective factors that hinder or foster recovery along with the rehabilitative measures that ensures recovery among alcohol abusers. The main objective is to understand the status of recovering addict along with the risk and protective factors that support their recovery. The study has undergone extensive literature review to understand the problem of addiction among youth. In addition to the literature, preliminary data is also collected from the recovering youth and counselors to understand the recovery process of an individual. The study is qualitative in nature where 15 in-depth interviews were conducted. Purposive sampling technique was used. Data are mostly primary in nature though secondary literature was reviewed. Findings depict significant results that satisfy the objectives of the study. The Ecological perspective provided a considerable platform to understand the relationship of an individual towards a society in large in a recovery process. Although there is onset of risk in every outlook, the 12 step programme in every rehabilitation centre's proved to be significant in creating a protective shield in moulding the problematic behavior among addicts.

Keywords: Alcoholism, youth, recovery, rehabilitation.

Psychosocial Function and Mental Health among Medical Students

Neetu Sheokand[1], Pradeep Kumar [2]

[1]M.Phil Psychiatric Social Work Scholar, [2]Consultant Psychiatric Social Work,
State Institute of Mental Health, University of Health Sciences, Rohtak, Haryana, Email: sheokandneetu@gmail.com

The medical curriculum is known to be one of the most stressful curriculum all over the world. There have been various reports that suggested that the medical student face multiple symptoms of stress and their psychosocial adjustment is also poor. Aims: To assess the Psychosocial function and mental health of medical student. Tools: Here in this study we have administered Symptom Check List-90-Revised (SCL-90-R) and Global Adjustment Scale (GAS) on medical, humanities and commerce undergraduates (N=100 in each group) with aim to tap the symptoms of psychological stress and adjustment problems. Methodology: The study was comparative and cross sectional. The students were chosen randomly. Informed written consent was obtained before assessment from each participant. Statistics: The students two tailed "t" test. Chi squared test and Pearson's correlation were applied wherever applicable. Results and conclusion: The results suggest that medical students were better adjusted, less stressed in comparison with humanities and commerce group of students. Our findings are unique and little bit different from the previous studies.

Keywords: Student, Mental Health, Psychosocial, Family, Emotion

Impact of Coping Styles and Resources and Academic Aspirations on the Psychological Wellbeing in School Going Adolescents

Neha Roy[1], D.Ram[2], Vani Narula[3], Dipanjan Bhattacharjee [4]

[1]Ph.D Scholar, Dept. of Social Work, Jamia Millia Islamia University, New Delhi.
[2]Director & Professor of Psychiatry, CIP, Ranchi.
[3]Associate Professor, Dept. of Social Work, Jamia Millia Islamia University, New Delhi.
[4]Assistant Professor of Department of Psychiatric Social Work, CIP, Ranchi
Email: neha.roy24@yahoo.com

Background: Adolescence represents a period of intensive growth and change in nearly all aspects of child's physical, mental, social and emotional life. Coping encompasses the cognitive and behavioural strategies which individuals use both to manage a stressful situation and the negative emotional reactions elicited by that event. Adolescent students face unparalleled pressure and challenges with society's current emphasis on academic perfection. Psychological well-being is a state of mind desirable for one and all. Well-being includes health in social, physical, mental, emotional, career, and spiritual domains. Aim: To examine the relationship between coping styles and resources, academic aspirations and subjective well-being of school going adolescents. Method: The study had been conducted at 3 Senior Secondary Schools (3 schools) of the city of Ranchi. It was a cross-sectional school based study. Sample size was 120 (60 boys and 60 girls) who were attending Class X, XI & XII. Purposive sampling was used for data collection. The tools used were Socio-demographic clinical data sheet, Ways of Coping Questionnaire, Academic Motivation Scale- High School Version and Satisfaction with Life Scale. Statistical measures like independent samples t' test, and 'chi-square' test and Pearson's correlation-coefficient were used. It was administered on the samples and data was analyzed using SPSS 20 version. Result: Results and Implications will be discussed during the time of presentation.

Keywords: Coping Styles and Resources, Academic Aspirations, Subjective Well-being

Patient Satisfaction Regarding Quality of Hospital Services in Cardiology Outpatient Department in a Tertiary Care Government Hospital, South India

Ramaraju Jayalakshmi[1], Subitha Lakshminarayanan[2], Santhosh Satheesh[1]

[1]Departments of Cardiology, [2]Department of Preventive & Social Medicine, JIPMER, Pondicherry, Email: nishkalan2005@gmail.com

Background: Patient satisfaction is an established yardstick to measure the effectiveness of health care delivery. Studies on health care quality and patient satisfaction provide input to health planners about lacunae in the existing health services. Aim: To assess factors associated with the level of patient satisfaction in coronary artery disease (CAD) outpatients (OPD) from the Cardiology department of a tertiary care hospital in South India. Methods: This cross sectional study included 388 adults attending cardiology OPD using Simple Random Sampling. Structured exit interviews were conducted using a validated Performa. Socio-demographic parameters, clinical profile, quality of services and patient's satisfaction was assessed using Patients Satisfaction Questionnaire (PSQ-18). Results: Majority(n=255,65.7%) belonged to 35-54 age group, 70.6%(274) were males,56%(218) were in 'upper lower' socio economic class, 68%(265)had health insurance.60% had Chronic Stable Angina,95%(367)underwent outpatient coronary angiogram (CAG)Quality of Service: 83% reported very clear direction to OPD, doctors, and Laboratory services. Drug advice by doctor was very clear for 81%. Among the patients who underwent OPD CAG, very clear understanding was reported by 78% for the procedure, 87% for potential risk and complications. Pre-procedure precautions were very clear for 77% and post procedure 88%. Cleanliness was rated as good by 87% for toilets, 86% for dining room and 97% for waiting area. Availability of drinking water was rated poor by 48%. Facility for overnight stay was rated average by 74%.Patient Satisfaction: Overall Patient Satisfaction score was 84 (IQR 82-87). It was comparable for age, sex, domicile and socioeconomic status. Satisfaction was better among free treatment in comparison to paid and insurance patients ($p<0.01$). Conclusion: Patient satisfaction among outpatient CAD patients was good in this tertiary care government hospital frequented by upper lower class. It is affected by the mode of payment for services but not socioeconomic class. Drinking water and overnight stay facilities need to be improved.

Keywords: Coronary Artery Disease, Outpatient, Patient satisfaction, PSQ-18

Impact of Non-Pharmacological Interventions in the Community Based Treatment of Substance Abuse in a Resettlement Colony, Sunder Nagari, Delhi

Ratnesh Kumar

Sup.MSSO NDDTC, AIIMS, Delhi, Email: ratnesh.aiims@gmail.com

Background: There are individuals who are engaged in substance abuse, afflicted families and vulnerable groups who may not be able to avail the de-addiction facilities on account of difficulty in access, social stigma and other factors. The Community based treatment approach of substance abuse is a key strategy to reach out the above clients and help them to ensure the treatment compliance using various approaches. Combination of pharmacological and non-pharmacological interventions is generally more effective in the management of substance abuse patients. Aim of the Study: The main aim of this study is to explore and assess the compliance and regularity in follow-ups of the community based treatment for substance abuse and also to highlight the impact of various non-pharmacological interventions to manage the non-compliance. Methods: The records of 164 clients were scrutinized and the semi-structured interview was conducted among the 146 clients coming to Mobile Clinic at Sunder Nagari to avail the treatment for substance abuse. Purposive sampling technique is used. Results: The result shows an alarming number of drop-outs were 51% which is because of migration, involvement in anti-social/illegal activities (which leads to incarnation) and death. The irregularity in treatment is 3% because of lack of family involvement, lack of motivation, influence of peer group. The main reasons behind drop out are migration (15%) and involvement in illegal activities like pick pocketing (50%). However 30%

of the patients are regular as they are integrated with the family. In case they are relapsed their family members were contacted and it helped in resuming of the treatment. 17 patients started working in the needle-syringe exchange program of NACO as a peer educator and daily wage earner. Rest were provided occupational guidance and motivated to get employment near the centre. All of the regular patients were attending the sessions of Non-pharmacological interventions like-*Individual Counseling,* Motivational Enhancement Therapy, RP Sessions and Occupational Rehabilitation from the experts on regular basis. Conclusion: Overall it is concluded that the non-pharmacological interventions are very effective in the substance abuse clients for the better prognosis.

Keywords: Substance abuse, non-pharmacological interventions, *Individual Counseling,* Motivational Enhancement Therapy, Occupational Rehabilitation, incarnation

Quality of Life among Female Elderly Living in Old Age Home and Community

Rishi Panday[1] Pradeep Kumar[2]

[1]Ph.D. Scholar, Department of Social Work, Jamia Millia Islamia, New Delhi,
[2]Consultant, Psychiatric Social Work Unit,
State Institute of Mental Health, PGIMS, University of Health Sciences, Rohtak, Email: rishiraj.lu@gmail.com

Background: Female elderly faced many difficulties in daily life style that are living in old age home and community. Social workers can be found in a wide variety of practice setting in field of ageing. The role of the social worker is often unique in theses setting as social work's primary focus is the psychosocial well-being of the female elderly. Aim: To assess and compare relationship of Quality of life among female elderly living in old age home and community. Methods and Materials: A cross sectional research design was adopted for the study. Sixty samples were recruited through purposive sampling technique, thirty samples from old age homes and thirty samples from community. Tools such as socio-demographic data sheet, Quality of Life scale were administered to obtain the data. Result and Conclusion: Findings of this study indicate that female elderly living in old age home had better quality of life in compare to elderly female living with family setup. Based on the present study finding Psycho-social intervention programme be developed to enhancing Quality of Life of female elderly persons.

Keywords: Old age home, Ageing and Quality of Life

Assessment of the Scope for Social Work Intervention for the Effective Utilization of Janani Shishu Suraksha Karyakram: KAP Study amongst Post-natal women in Sub Centre Dighi-Jikthan, District Aurangabad

Rosy Joseph[1], Sanjay Bhonge[2], Rajaram Gavade[3], Kalpna Pandit[4] & Deepak Raut[5]

[1]PHNO, [2]SW, [3]SA, [4]ANM,[5]Director. FWTRC, Mumbai, Email: bhongesanjay@gmail.com

Introduction: Social Work at community level can bridge the gap between the service delivery and the Beneficiaries. They can create awareness, mobilize and ensure the utilization of services at health facilities. Government of India initiated several programs to improve the institutional deliveries with the goal of reducing maternal mortality. Janani Shishu Suraksha Karyakram was launched to reduce out of pocket expenses and to encourage the institutional delivery of all pregnant women in the public sector facilities under the overall umbrella of NRHM. Aim of the study: To understand the scope for community based social work interventions by assessing the level of awareness, availability and utilization of JSSK amongst PNC mothers at Sub-centre Dighi-Jikthan, Aurangabad District. Methods: The cross sectional study was conducted in February 2017, at SC, Dighi Jikthan, Dist. Aurangabad, Maharashtra. A Semi structured Interview Schedulewas used to assess KAP of JSSK entitlements. Around 40 post-natal womenwere selected, who delivered in last six months. Analysis was done using Excel &SPSS at 5% level of Significance. Result: Mean age of the respondents was 25.2 years and minimum was 20 years. Most of the respondents were high school education 16(40%). Average Monthly income of the respondent's families was Rs. 4877.50 only. All respondent were aware of the about 10 entitlements out of the 13 provided under the JSSK. Most of the 21(52%) mothers were aware about free diet. Only 2 (5%) mothers were known about free blood transfusion facility if required during delivery. None of the mothers were aware that even their sick infant is entitled to receive free blood if needed. The utilization statistics shows that,34 (85%)ANC registered and delivered under JSSK in govt facility. However only12 (30%) received free drug and consumables. Conclusion: This shows that though there is good awareness level of JSSK amongs Postnatal mother, utilization of services available free of cost were not satisfactory. Social work interventions have a wider scope at the community level as an educator, Counselloer, motivator and catalyst for the demand generation and utilization of the JSSK services by the ANC and PNC mothers. To acomplish the objective of RMNCHA+ program, i.e. safe delivery and reduction of MMR, NMR, IMR.

Keywords: JSSK, ANC, PNC, Social Work Interventions

Severity of Violence and Quality Of Life of Women with Psychiatric Illness as Compared to Normal Controls

Sapna Kumari[1], Manisha Kiran[2], S. Choudhary[3]

[1]Consultant, Air Force Hospital, Barmer ,Rajasthan, [2]Associate Professor & Head, Department of Psychiatric Social Work, RINPAS, Kanke, Ranchi, [3]Professor, D r. D.Y. Patil Medical College, Pune.
Email:sapsin2@gmail.com

Background: Women are principal providers of care and support to families. Yet every social indicator shows a fundamental social inequality (Sharma, 2000). Materials & Method: This was a cross-sectional study designed to assess and compare the severity of violence and quality of life of women with psychiatric illness and normal controls. Based on purposive sampling technique a sample consisting of 120 subjects were selected from in-patient (female ward) and out-patient services of the Ranchi Institute of Neuro-Psychiatry and Allied Sciences and Kanke Area. Both groups were matched on socio-demographic details. Normal controls were screened using GHQ-12 (Goldberg and William, 1978). Severity of Violence against Women Scales (Marshall, 1992a), The Revised Conflict Tactics Scale (Straus et. al, 1996) and WHOQOL-BREF scale (Hindi version) (Saxena et. al., 1998) were used. Results: The study showed that except in symbolic violence, threats of moderate and serious violence as well psychological aggression there was significant difference found in other dimensions of violence and their level of severity in both the groups. Conclusion: The study has been able to identify the group who are at increased risk of violence but at the same time it was also found that women with psychiatric illness as well as normal controls faced various forms of violence equally although both the groups differed in the level of severity. It was also found that normal controls had better quality of life.

Keywords: Violence, Quality of life

Knowledge and Awareness Regarding Fertility and Reproductive Factors, Their Association with Socio Economic Status Among Indian Women

Shobha Kandpal, Monika Gupta, Reeta Mahey, P. Vanamail, Neena Malhotra, Neeta Singh, Alka Kriplani

All India Institute of Medical Sciences, New Delhi, New Delhi,
Email: shobha_kandpal@rediffmail.com

Objective: To evaluate the awareness regarding limits of reproduction in relation to female age, menstrual cycle and treatment options including the need for assisted reproductive technique &their association with socio economic status. Methods: Cross-sectional study of 205 infertile patients seeking treatment for infertility at our assisted reproduction unit between March 17 - August 2017 were interviewed. Results: Majority of women (59%) belonged to the age group of 20-30 years indicating a young age group in need of infertility evaluation. More than half (63%) of the patients were from the middle socio-economic strata. Even so knowledge about fertility and reproduction was low: 85% missed the ovulatory period in the menstrual cycle, only 8% considered age more than 35 years as the most significant risk factor for infertility. Approximately 60-80% was not aware when to seek treatment for infertility after trying for pregnancy. Patients also had limited knowledge regarding artificial reproductive technique and need for donor acolytes (egg taken from another woman) in advanced age group. Conclusion: There is significant gap in knowledge and awareness regarding the fertile period and effect of ageing on infertility. This can be improved by informal education starting from first visit till they satisfied with the adequate knowledge on the above aspects. Patients are encouraged with positive attitude to have a baby with available modern techniques and they were satisfied with their gain on knowledge about the available option.

Keywords: Knowledge, Awareness, Fertility, Reproductive and Indian Women

The Role of Mental Health Intervention in Gender Affirmative Therapy

Srabasti Majumdar

Research Scholar, School of women's Studies, Jadavpur University.
Email: srabastee@gmail.com

This paper will focus on the mental health issues and the role of a medical psychiatric social worker and counsellor during the transition of transgender individuals undergoing gender affirmative therapy. The domain of gender expression is vast, and hence cannot be defined and made limited. The transgender individuals often wish to transform their anatomy in an effort to harmonize their gender identity with their physical existence, to come out of the painful existence of being "trapped in the wrong body" by breaking the linear relationship between sex and the ascribed gender. Transsexual individuals who have already gone through 'Sex Reassignment Surgery' have to adjust to the 'new desired body'. Gender Affirmative Therapy is a life changing process and is irreversible. It has many stages and procedures involved in it. These processes give the transgender individuals the opportunity to materialize their 'dreams' of inhabiting their 'preferred' body but at the same time the process is long, arduous and quite expensive and thus can cause a lot of stress and mental health issues. They have to face challenges, social stigma, ostracization and alienation. In this whole process the mental health professional stays beside the transgender individual as a part of her/his/zer emotional support system and this paper will discuss the crucial role of the social worker providing mental health support during gender affirmative therapy.

Keywords: Mental Health, Gender Affirmative Therapy

ग्रामीण युवा महिलाओं को यौन प्रजनन शिक्षा की आवश्यकता

संगीता वार्ष्णेय

एम. एस. डब्लू, यूपी. यू.एम.एस. सैफई, ई-मेल-varsangeeta@gmail-com

पृष्ठभूमि (Backround)- हमारे देश मे यौनिकता एवं प्रजनन संबंधी मुद्दे समुदाय में प्रायः अचर्चित रहते है।50% युवाओ का विवाह कम उम्र में हो जाता है।युवाओ को अपनी लैंगिकता समझने के लिए जानकारी एवं सेवाएं उपलब्ध करानी चाहिए ताकि वे यौन और प्रजनन के मामले में परस्पर जिम्मेदारी की भावना के लिए वे तैयार हो सके। उद्देश्य(objective)- प्रजनन स्वास्थ्य आवश्यकताओ पर समाज की सहयोगी प्रतिक्रिया ऐसी जानकारी पर आधारित होनी चाहिए जिससे जिम्मेदारी पूर्ण निर्णय लेने के लिए उनमे परिपक्वता आ सके। सामग्री और तरीका (Material and methods) -ग्रामीण क्षेत्र(परियोजना क्षेत्र आगरा) में यह अध्ययन 20 गाँव की 300 युवतियों पर की गयी है। त्तम जमेजमक`मउप`जतनबजनतमक च्मतवितउं युवतियों के इंटरव्यू के लिए प्रयुक्त किया गया। परिणाम(तमेनसज)- 15&19वर्ष की उम्र में लगभग 50%युवतियों का विवाह कम उम्र में हो जाता है।जिसमे 41% का 19 वर्ष तक व 9%का 14 वर्ष तक की अवस्था तक विवाह हो जाता है। 57%विवाहित महिलाये 13&19वर्ष की उम्र तक गर्भधारण कर लेती है। 85% महिलायें बिना ज्ञान के ही गर्भधारण कर लेती है। निष्कर्ष -कई प्रकार की सरकारी तथा गैर सरकारी संस्थाओं के इस दिशा में कार्य करने के वावजूद ग्रामीण उत्तरप्रदेश की युवतियों को यौन सम्बन्धो में समानता, उन पर हो रहे अत्याचार जिम्मेदारी पूर्ण यौन व्यवहार, परिवार नियोजन पद्यति,पारिवारिक जीवन संबंधी शिक्षा और परामर्श के लिए उपयुक्त कार्यक्रम तैयार करे ताकि वे डर, संकोच व भय रहित अपना जीवन व्यतीत कर सके।

संकेत शब्द (Keywords): यौनिकता, प्रजनन, लेंगिकता, यौन, काउंसलिंग।

Effects of Strength Based Supportive Therapy on Family Functioning and Coping among Persons with Alcohol Dependence Syndrome

Shrikant Pawar[1], Niteen Abhivant[2], Praful Kapse[3], Manisha Kiran[4], Amool R Singh[5]

[1]Lecturer, Maharastra Institute of Mental Health, Pune, Maharastra, India
[2]Associate Professor, Dept. of Psychiatry, B. J. Govt. Medical College, Pune.
[3]Mental Health Specialist, Sir Ratan Tata Trust & Navajbai Ratan Tata Trust, Mumabi
[4]Associate Professor & Head, Dept. of Psychiatric Social Work, RINPAS, Kanke, Ranchi
[5]Professor, Dept. of Clinical Psychology, RINPAS, Kanke, Ranchi
Email: shrikant.pawar55@gmail.com

Background: Alcohol dependence is a complex behavior with far-reaching harmful effects on the family, work, society, as well as on the physical and mental health of the individual. Epidemiological studies conducted in India showed that 20-30% of our population is using alcohol at a harmful level. Mental health professionals provide support and understanding of the illness for the affected individual and family members. They work together on planning treatment, provide mutual support and understanding of the disorder. Aim: To study the effects of strength based supportive therapy on family functioning and coping of persons with alcohol dependence syndrome. Methodology: This was a hospital based intervention study. It had adopted the quasi experimental before and after with control group research design. Participants were randomly allocated to the experimental and control groups. 10 persons with alcohol dependence syndrome were selected for the study five each alcohol dependent syndrome individuals and their family members were assigned in the control group (treatment as usual group; TAU) and five alcohol dependent syndrome individuals and their family members were assigned in the experimental group (treatment as usual + family intervention group). Family functioning was assessed through McMaster family assessment device Patients were assessed through brief cope Result: The study results indicated significant improvement in various domains of family functioning in experimental group participants compared to the treatment as usual group. It has also noted improvement in coping among patients. Conclusion: strength based supportive intervention useful for the caregivers as well as it also helpful in improving coping among person with alcohol dependence syndrome.

Keywords: Strength based supportive therapy, Alcohol dependence, Caregivers.

Globalization and Promotion of Tobacco Product at Point of Purchase: A Public Health Issue

Viney Dhiman

Medical Social Worker, Department of Cardiology, PGIMER, Chandigarh.
Email: viney.pu@gmail.com

Background of the Study: Tobacco is at the centre of the contradictions inherent in the evolving process of globalization. It is where the goals of a set of multinationals are clearly in conflict with public health and welfare and where globalization of values such as accountability and corporate responsibility are under severe pressure. The transformation of marketing and promotion of harmful commodities, such as tobacco products, is one important component of globalized public health threats. The industry looks towards the creation of new brands, products and variety in the market. Today's youth is attracted to such a flavored product which is dressed up with brightly colors and attractive packing. Given the harmful influence of tobacco advertising and promotion on current, potential, and former smokers, marketing regulation is a necessary component in the effort to combat the global tobacco epidemic. Objectives: The current paper provides a general review of emerging promotional channels, such as packaging, viral marketing. Secondly analyzes the various dimensions of tobacco globalization as a barrier to sustainable development. Methodology: The research consisted observational information and descriptive design in nature. Observations like display of advertisement, variety of smoked and smokeless tobacco products and use of any promotion were noted. The information was collected from tobacco vendors of Bathinda, Gurdaspur and Jalandhar City based on Convenience sampling. These included temporary kiosk, permanent kiosk and permanent shops. Results: The results of the present study illustrate that cigarette & bidi packs and smokeless tobacco products were carried out the flavored properties, with catching tag lines, attractive packaging and lastly dull warning images on the packs of both segments, advertised at point of purchase locally. Number of flavored, foreign, Indian brand and locally manufactured cigarettes packs were available and sold at point of purchase. These products with attractive packing packages attract the young population and these approaches leads to lifetime addiction and affected with tobacco related diseases.

Keywords: Globalization, Tobacco Industry, Products, Kiosk, Vendors

and leisure activities (Primary disability). The illness is chronic in nature and recurrent and causes education and vocational training delay and discontinued (secondary Disability). Social factors like discrimination and stigma prevent people with mental health problem from giving employment (tertiary disability). Psychiatric rehabilitation or (psycho-social rehabilitation) enables persons with MI to develop to the fullest extent of their capacities despite the existence of mental illness. Psycho -social intervention is a process that deals with a broad range of psycho- social problems and promotes the restoration of social cognition And infrastructure as well as the independence and dignity of individual and groups. It serves to prevent pathological development and further social dislocation. The main techniques of psycho-social intervention are helping the individual, ventilating their emotion, active listening, showing empathy, helping them to externalize their interest, building the social support. The intervention should be holistic because it means emotional support and also practical help, suggestions, guidance, providing information and education. The focus is on the identification of needs and attention to specific problems related to areas like medical facility, legal aid, lively hood, housing etc. psychosocial intervention is done by using all the methods, techniques and skills of Psychiatric- social work that includes patient education, supportive therapy, group intervention, family intervention, breaking bad news, community re entry training , addressing disability benefit, unknown patients services, pre-discharge counseling, and rehabilitation.

Keywords: Psychosocial Rehabilitation, Mental Health

Social Medicine and Social Sciences

Jagpreet Singh

MSW, Dept. of Community Medicine, GMCH, Chandigarh.
Email: jagpreetmatta14@gmail.com

This paper is describing the manner in which disease may cause from, social problems and how public health or social medicine efforts may contribute to their solution.

Objective of Social Medicine: Identify social determinants of health and disease

- Devise mechanisms for alleviating suffering and ill health through social policies and action.
- Social, cultural, psychological and behavioral factors are important variables in the etiology, prevalence and distribution of disease.
- The way the people live, their habits, beliefs, values and customs are significant determinants of individual and collective health.
- The behavioral sciences have made significant role in developing better understanding about the social etiology of health problems.
- Sociology, Social Psychology, Cultural Anthropology.

Keywords: Social Medicine. Social Sciences

Study on Impact of Counseling Interventions with Multi Drug-Resistant Tuberculosis Patients

Amandeep Singh[1], Manjit Kaur[2]

[1]Research Scholar, [2]Research Associate

Social work is a profession primarily concerned with the remedy to psycho-social problems and deficiencies which exists in the relationship between the individual and his social environment. TB1 is one of among the major health problem, which has been killed number of lives in history and also effecting current health conditions, worldwide. This infection has a close relationship with immune system and people with low immunity are in more risk. The symptoms of active TB of the lung are coughing, sometimes with sputum or blood, chest pains, weakness, weight loss, fever and night sweats are common among all its types. MDR-TB2 infection may be classified as either primary or acquired. Primary MDR-TB occurs in patients who have not previously been infected with TB but who become infected with a strain that is resistant to treatment. Treatment for MDR-TB is long and carries significant side effects that make treatment adherence difficult for the patients. Though the WHO3 has recommended a shorter treatment regimen4 for MDR-TB, patients in India are still being treated under the previous regimen, which can last up to 24 months. The first six to nine months of treatment are particularly intensive, with the patient requiring daily injections and up to 13 tablets a day. People MDR-TB in low-income countries face many problems during treatment and cure rates are low. The purpose of the study was to identify and document the problems experienced by peoples receiving care for MDR-TB and how they cope when support is not provided, to estimate the effectiveness of counselling on treatment. This study had focused on the impact of counselling given to patient with and after medicine. It is found that counseling is a tool which is very useful to make patients healthy & Socially- Economically Developed.

Keywords: Tuberculosis, Multi Drug Resistance, World Health Organization

Overview of Slum Intervention Programme

Gurpreet Singh[1], *Jagtar Singh[1], Priya Rani[1]

[1]Executive Members AAS Welfare Society, Punjab Email: jagtardamdiwal62@gmail.com

Aim of the present study is to explore the socio-economic issues faced by the slum dwellers in Malerkotla and see the efficacy of the solutions implemented with the help of local administration. It was an exploratory study and sample consisted of one person each from 100 consecutive households in the study area. Inclusion criteria included participants of any age, any gender and not having any severe physical disability. Households which were locked were not included in the survey. After obtaining the informed consent, survey questionnaire prepared by the researchers was administered. Data obtained were analysed qualitatively. To address the needs in the area of education, sanitation and cleanliness; enrolment of children dropped out of school, free medical camps, providing water tank, cleanliness drive and distribution of free clothes was done to deal with problem at hand.

Keywords: Slum Dwellers, Problems Faced, Intervention

Social Work Intervention in Promotion of Health

Ankur Saxena [1], Sneha Chandrapal [2]

[1]Professor, Faculty of Social Work, M.S. University, Vadodara, Gujarat,
[2]Research Scholar, Department of Social Work, S.P. University, V.V. Nagar, Gujarat
Email: ankur.a.saxena@gmail.com

Social work is a form of professional service to the people, containing a composite of knowledge and skills, attempting at supporting them, as individuals or groups, for obtaining satisfying relationships and standards of life in harmony with their particular wishes and capacities and in accordance with those of community. Social workers in their professional capacity probably have more contact with the medical services of the community than with any other single resource. Certainly this is true of the case worker whose functions include working with individuals, many of whom have health problems. Reciprocally, social work makes direct contributions to the medical profession. The constant growth, demands, and changes in health care have had a serious impact on the viability and need for social workers in all areas and settings of health care. Social workers are regularly involved when a person's health is impacted by complex social, psychological, family and institutional dynamics. Furthermore, in their commitment to self-determination, social workers ensures that individuals within the health care system have access to information and are able to make decisions concerning their health and wellbeing. Social workers present distinct and valuable contribution in providing suitable and targeted services to meet the complex needs of patients, families and communities within the health care field. This present paper highlights social work intervention in health care, role of social worker in the field of health care, scope of practice in health social work.

Keywords: Social Work, Health Care, Intervention

Corporate Social Responsibility and Women's Health Prevention and Promotion - A Study of CSR Initiatives of a Public Sector Undertaking

Ashvini Kumar Singh

Assistant Professor, Department of Social Work, Jamia Millia Islamia, New Delhi,
Email: ashvinisw@gmail.com

Improving the health status of women requires improved use of preventive health care services and health care behaviors. Use of preventive health care services is central to improving the long-term health status of women. To enhance the availability and use of preventive services for women, it is important to understand women's unique health care requirements. Women are more likely than men have difficulty in accessing health care services due to various reasons. (NHCM). Contemporary business philosophy assumes that an organization has to be responsible for its actions and deeds vis-a-vis all the actors in its environment. An organization's achievement of business excellence requires a fully developed corporative social responsibility. In order for domestic enterprises to become competitive on the international level, it is necessary to change ways of thinking and to adopt contemporary global standards in the area of organization management. The application of the concept of corporate social responsibility is one of the basic prerequisites for the achievement of business excellence on the part of domestic enterprises. The paper tries to understand the relevance of CSR activities and their role in women's health prevention and promotion; it tries to understand how CSR efforts through legislative measures are helping to address the issues related women's health prevention and promotion women in contemporary time. While deliberating on interventions made by NTPC Badarpur a public sector unit and their impact on women's health prevention and promotion the paper also argues that if women are provided appropriate health prevention and promotion services the problems related to women health can be addressed to a great extent. Paper has also given many suggestions and recommendations to strengthen the CSR activities for women's health prevention and promotion.

Keywords: Women's health prevention and promotion, CSR, health care services, health care behaviors.

Exploring the conspicuous relation between child survival and human development in India

Asiya Nasreen

Assistant Professor, Department of Social Work, Jamia Millia Islamia, New Delhi
Email: anasreen@jmi.ac.in

Health is an important determinant of human development. It has remained a matter of concern for people of all age groups and in all times. The health and well being status of children is measured by way of Infant Mortality Rate (IMR).Child Health was an important health goal of erstwhile Millennium Development Goals and of presently operational Sustainable development Goals (2016-2030). Still, statistics of Ministry of Women and Child Development indicate the still IMR is 45 per live births which is higher than other Asian counterparts. High mortality among children is a blow to the human development due to wastage of critical human resource. The paper examines the situation of child survival in India, the cultural practices that prevent people to turn their back from health care facilities for infant care and the implications on human development. Findings suggests that cultural practices are given prominence and people fail to access immediate care for new born that puts at stake child survival and compromise with agenda of human development. Thus, time has come to change harmful cultural practices as well as the mindset of people towards adopting healthy child care practices as little steps towards realization of sustainable health goal targets and overall improving the state of human development.

Keywords: Exploring, conspicuous relation, child survival and human development

Depression and Stress among Older Adults residing in Old Age Home

Avinash Verma[1], Prashant Srivastava[2]

[1]Social Worker, Dept. of Psychiatry, GMCH, Chandigarh

[2]Psychiatric Social Work,
Dept. of Psychiatry, Kalpana Chawla Government Medical College and Hospital, Karnal, Haryana.
Email: avinashgmch2014@gmail.com

Background: Ageing is inevitable. It is irreversible, progressive and is associated with decline in functions. The individual gradually becomes dependent physically, functionally, socially and economically. Older Adults usually exhibit multiple health problems with complex interactions. Elderly people residing in old age home have a feeling of depression extreme level of stress, hopelessness, helplessness and worthlessness. Now a day's most of the elderly people are isolated from families. Objective: This study was planned to assess the Depression and Stress among Older Adults residing in Old Age Home in Gender Perspective and to see the association between Depression and Stress among Older Adults residing in Old Age Home. Sample: 60 Older Adults (30 Male Older Adults residing in Old Age Home and 30 Female Older Adults residing in Old Age Home) were included who were qualified the inclusion and exclusion criteria based on Purposive Sampling technique. Design: In present study cross sectional design was used. Tools: They were evaluated on Beck Depression Inventory and Perceived Stress Scale. Result and Conclusion: The result and conclusion will be discussed during presentation.

Keywords: Depression, Stress, Older Adults.

Brief Intervention with Caregivers of People Living with Schizophrenia

Bhupendra Singh[1], Priti Singh[2]

[1]Assistant Professor, Psychiatric Social Work [2]Professor, Psychiatry,
Institute of Mental Health, Pt. BD Sharma University of Health Sciences, Rohtak
Email: 33bhupendrasingh@gmail.com

Introduction: Families constitute a primary source of care for people with mental illness but often face extensive trouble in fulfilling their role. Family psychoeducational interventions have been developed to address these problems with established efficacy and effectiveness. Psychoeducation of patients and families seems to be a useful first step in the psychological treatment of schizophrenia. However, the content and dimensions of efficacy of well-structured family psychoeducation have not yet been established. Aim: The present study was planned to assess the effectiveness of brief intervention with caregivers in improving family cohesion, alleviating caregivers' burden, and reducing depression anxiety and stress in relatives of those suffering from schizophrenia. Methods: 214 family members of the admitted patients in Institute of Mental Health, Pt. B. D. Sharma UHS, Rohtak, with a diagnosis of schizophrenia, in the year of 2016, were included in the study. On the basis of random assignment 54 received intervention, and 54 were taken as the control (treatment as usual) group. Self structured socio-demographic datasheet, Family Burden Scale, and DASS were administered to the subjects. Informed consent was sought from the patients and their caregivers as well. Result: Family Psychoeducation showed positive effect in the area of understanding and knowledge, objective and subjective family burden, it also decreased the depression, anxiety and stress throughout the study period. Family psychoeducation constitutes a valuable non stigmatizing intervention that empowers relatives of people with severe mental illness and enables them to cope effectively with the illness.

Keywords: Family, Group Psychoeducation, Schizophrenia, Stress

Professional Social Worker's Voice towards Overcoming Challenges in Hospital Settings: A Qualitative Study

Deepalatha R. Shetty[1], **Krishan Kumar**[2]

[1]TISS, Mumbai [2]PGIMER, Chandigarh. Email: 90deepu@gmail.com

Professional Social work is accepted as one of the helping profession in all over the world, and it is still in a growing stage in India. PSWs work in different settings, but current study mainly emphasis towards the hospital setting. PSWs are experts in dealing individual, groups and social issues through mobilizing resources, information and enable to overcome their problems. They also promote psycho-social intervention to their client and arrange session with their family. They work in a multidisciplinary team medical as well non-medical staffs. PSWs perform different roles within as well as outside the hospital set up for health care and rehabilitation. As we know profession is in developing stage, they face several difficulties in day to day professional life. Present study adopted a qualitative approach to deeply understand the difficulties of PSWs and ways to overcome from their challenges. For exploring information in-depth interviews were conducted in two government medical institutes situated at urban city of North India. Present paper emphasis on the ways of dealing their problems in hospital settings and advise for future to avoid such difficulties. Even this paper attempts to illustrate the importance of various views given by participants to overcome their challenges. It arouses the need for addressing PSWs challenges in hospital settings as well provides further ideas how these challenges can be overcome.

Keywords: Professional Social Worker, Hospital, Challenges and Overcoming

Challenges among Social Workers in Hospital Settings: A Qualitative Study on Role Confusion

Deepalatha R. Shetty[1], **Krishan Kumar**[2]

[1]TISS Mumbai, [2]PGIMER, Chandigarh. Email: 90deepu@gmail.com

Social workers with their specialized skills and training are capable to intervene individuals, groups, community and various institutions level in problem solution. This study mainly focuses on hospital social work. In hospital setting they play very important role to help the patients to help themselves through counseling, psycho-education, therapies, emotional support, facilitator and mediator through contributing towards the strengthening of health care system. Rendering service in hospital is a satisfying job for social workers in terms of helping patients and families in addressing issues and coping up with illness. But in India this is growing profession, so role of SW is not clear in many settings, hospital setting is one out of those settings. In hospital settings, Social worker works as a member of treating teams, in different multispecialty department. Present study adopted a qualitative approach to deeply understand the challenges faced by PSWs. For exploring information in-depth interviews were conducted in two government medical institutes situated at urban city of North India. Most of the participant reported role of SW is not clear in institution. Some of told they are just used for clerical work for filling up of papers, some of were kept for account keeping, store keeping, in library, data entry etc. This paper will give clear picture of social work profession in hospital setting.

Keywords: Social Work, Challenges, Hospital, Social work profession, Role Blurring

Challenge Resolutions among Social Workers in Hospital Settings: A Qualitative Study Deepalatha

Deepalatha R. Shetty

Mphil, Scholar, TISS Mumbai. Email: 90deepu@gmail.com

Professional Social work is accepted as one of the helping profession in all over the world, and it is still in a growing stage in India. PSWs work in different settings, but current study mainly emphasis towards the hospital setting. PSWs are experts in dealing individual, groups and social issues through mobilizing resources, information and enable to overcome their problems. They also promote psycho-social intervention to their client and arrange session with their family. They work in a multidisciplinary team medical as well non-medical staffs. PSWs perform different roles within as well as outside the hospital set up for health care and rehabilitation. As we know profession is in developing stage, they face several difficulties in day to day professional life. Present study adopted a qualitative approach to deeply understand the difficulties of PSWs and ways to overcome from their challenges. For exploring information in-depth interviews were conducted in two government medical institutes situated at urban city of North India. Present paper emphasis on the ways of dealing their problems in hospital settings and advise for future to avoid such difficulties. Even this paper attempts to illustrate the importance of various views given by participants to overcome their challenges. It arouses the need for addressing PSWs challenges in hospital settings as well provides further ideas how these challenges can be overcome.

Keywords: Professjional Social Worker, Hospital, Challenges and Overcoming

Marriage: Role and Contribution in Mental Illness

Divya Rai

M.Phil in Clinical Psychology, 1st year Trainee,
Department of Clinical Psychology, Amity, University Uttar Pradesh, Lucknow. Email: ddivirai@gmail.com

In Indian context marriage is a social institution of extreme relevance. Marriage plays an important role in mental health of an individual. Marriage does not always have positive outcome and the correlation between marriage and mental illness seems to be complicated. Major mental illnesses are usually diagnosed at late adolescent and early adulthood. This is the age when decision of marriage is taken, and this s rise to dilemma whether to marry or not, and whether marriage will improve or deteriorate the condition. The difficulties are equally faced by the individuals and their family members. Mental disorders and problems in marriage are closely linked though there is a controversy about it. In India, it is commonly assumed that marriage would help in the management of mental illness. Marriages are assumed to reduce the problems of individuals with mental illness through its effects on social support and intimate connection. But on the other hand, it has been seen that in most of the cases after marriage couples are separated or divorced due to mental illness and to some extent marriage contribute in the maintenance of mental illness. In this paper author wants to shed light on how marriage contributes to mental-health problems; whether it has a protective role; its outcome in major mental illnesses.

Keywords: Marriage, mental health, mental illness

Occupational Stress and Burn Out: A Study of Teachers in Special and General Schools

Hardeep Kaur[1], Laddi Singh[2]

[1]Assistant Professor, [2]Research Scholar, Department of Social Work, Punjabi University, Patiala.
Email: hardeepkaur66@gmail.com, laddikheri634@gmail.com

Background: Appropriate teaching skills are a significant part of a teacher's job. Even special educators are also required to create an atmosphere, flexible enough to house varied needs of their students. For the effective performance it is important to take into account the psychological well being of the teachers or else they may experience both stress and burnout. Objectives: This paper outlines the level of occupational stress and burn out amongst the teachers in general and special school .Sample: A total of

25 teachers each were taken up from the special school and a matching sample was selected from general schools .The teachers were matched on age and gender. Tools: Self constructed interview schedule was used to collect data on socio demographic profile of the teachers, Maslach Burnout Inventory (Christina Maslach and Susan E. Jackson 1981) and The Occupational Stress Index (Srivastava A.K. and Singh A P ,1981 were used . Results and Discussion: The results showed that under burn out, Emotional Exhaustion, Depersonalization were found to be significantly higher among teachers in special school and personal accomplishment was found to be lower. Scores on occupational stress indicated significant differences in the following sub scales of i.e role overload, unreasonable group & political pressure, responsibility of persons, unprofitability.

Keywords: Occupational Stress, Burn Out, Teachers

Adolescents in Orphanages: A Study of Academic Anxiety and School Adjustment

Hardeep Kaur[1], Arashmeet Chawla[2]

[1]Assistant Professor, [2]Research Scholar,Department of Social Work, Punjabi University, Patiala.
Email: hardeepkaur66@gmail.com

Background: Adolescence is a stage with tremendous pressure and stress and are expected to perform at every front, the main being academics. Academic anxiety is a feeling of being fearful, or stressed due to school pressures. School adjustment is a procedure that brings a person's behavior in compliance with the norms of the school, comprises of academic, social and emotional adjustment. Aims & Objectives: The present study aims to examine the level of academic anxiety and school adjustment among the school going adolescent girls and boys residing in orphanages and ones with their families. The gender differences will also examined. Sample: A total of 60 school going adolescent (girls and boys' aged 14-18 years) residing in orphanages and a controlled group of adolescents living with families matched on the basis of age, gender and school were selected for the study. Tools: Self constructed interview schedule to examine the socio demographic profile, Academic Anxiety Scale for Children by Dr. A.K. Singh and Dr. A. Sengupta and Adjustment Inventory for school students by A.K.P. Sinha and R.P.Singh were used. Results and Discussions: The results showed that the adolescents residing in orphanages had lower academic anxiety than the ones living with their families and scores of adolescent girls were higher than the boys .Results on school adjustment showed that the adolescents with families had significantly better school adjustment than the ones living in the orphanages and the girls had lower adjustment level than the boys.

Keywords: Adolescents, Orphanages, Academic anxiety, School adjustment.

Social Work Practices in Promotion of Organ Donation

Isha Goswami

MSW, Dept. of Social Work, Punjab University, Chandigarh Email: ishagoswami2794@gmail.com

Organ donation- a multi dimensional and a complex issue may have never been exposed to us in any way, whether that is in discussions with family or friends or from external communications and sources. With context to Indian population, people tend to feel uncomfortable talking about death and associated topics. Every 17 minutes, someone dies waiting for transplant and someone is added to a waiting list every 13 minutes in India. Organ donation and transplantation is permitted by law and is covered under the "Transplantation of Humans organs Act (THOA) 1994, which has allowed live and deceased organ donation. In 2011, the Amendment of the Act also brought in, donation of human tissues, thereby calling the Amended Act "Transplantation of Human organs and tissue ACT" 2011. As organ donation is often not within people's sphere of knowledge or experience, it is easy for people to distance themselves from the topic and keep it very low on the scale on matter of concern in their daily lives. A professional Social Worker/Transplant Coordinator can play a very vital role to increase the awareness in the community on the issue from conducting event health talks and group awareness sessions to rallies and nukkad nataks to increase sensitizations among the public. Moreover, conducting these activities would ultimately result into increased interest and participation of the people towards the cause.

Keywords: Social Work practice, Promotion, Organ Donation

Comparison of Life Events in Individuals with Bipolar Affective Disorder and Healthy Control

Jai Shanker Patel[1], **Manisha Kiran**[2]

[1]Ph. D Scholar, [2]Associate Professor & Head,
Department of Psychiatric Social Work, Ranchi Institute of Neuro-Psychiatry and Allied Sciences,
Kanke, Ranchi, Jharkhand Email:jspatel185@gmail.com

Background: There are so many theories explains the etiology of affective disorders, some of them emphasizing biological and others to psychological factors like personality, cognitive schemas, life events, etc.. The occurrence of psychiatric disorder cannot be understood by focusing on factors from a single domain only. Affective symptoms result from complex interactions between both environmental and biological factors and first one that have receive the more attention in this regard are life events. Aim: The present study aims to see the association between life events and development of affective disorders. Method: Thirty individuals diagnosed with bipolar affective disorders according to ICD-10 DCR will be select from the outpatient departments of RINPAS and thirty individuals using the purposive sampling technique. Tools: Hamilton Depression rating Scale and Young Mania Rating Scale will be used to assess the depressive and manic symptoms respectively. Life events will be assess by using presumptive stressful life events and PGI general well being will be use to assess the healthy control. Analysis: Appropriate statistical method will be applied by using SPSS version 20 Result: will be discussed at the time of presentation

Keywords: Bipolar Affective Disorder, Stressful Life Events and Healthy Control

Behaviour Problems in Children and Adolescents with Intellectual Disability and Functional Psychosis

Jagritee Singh[1], **Narendar Kumar Singh**[2]

[1]Ph.D scholar, Department of Social Work, Jamia Millia Islamia, New Delhi,
[2]P.S.W, Department of Psychiatric Social Work, Central Institute of Psychiatry, Ranchi.
Email: jagritisingh25@gmail.com

Background: Children with intellectual disability (ID) and functional psychosis are at heightened risk for behavior problems. Likewise, parents of children with ID and functional psychosis are more stressed than parents of typically developing children. Research on behavioral phenotypes suggests that different syndromes of ID and functional psychosis may be associated with distinct child behavioral risks. In the present study, parental reports of child behavior problems were examined for syndrome-specific differences. Aim & Objective: The purpose of this study was to assess and compare the behavior problems in children with intellectual disability and functional psychosis. Participants and Methods: This study was a cross-sectional hospital based study. The study samples were selected through purposive sampling technique. The sample size was 40 parents among which 20 parents of children and adolescent with intellectual disability and 20 parents of children and adolescent with functional psychosis taken from Erna Hoch Child and Adolescent Psychiatry Unit and Charak Outpatient Department, of the Central Institute of Psychiatry, Kanke, Ranchi. "Eyberg Child Behavior Inventory" (Eyberg S, Pincus D, 1999) scale was used for the data collection. Data were analysed by Statistical Package for Social Sciences (SPSS- 21 version). Result & Conclusion: Results will be discussed at the time of presentation.

Keywords: Intellectual Disability, Psychosis, Behaviors Problems

Stress and Care Giving Burden among Parents Having Children with Autism

Jyoti Kakkar[1], Prashant Srivastava[2]

[1]Professor, Dept of Social Work, Jamia Millia Islamia, New Delhi.
[2]Ph.D Scholar, Dept of Social Work, Jamia Millia Islamia, New Delhi and Psychiatric Social Worker, Dept. of Psychiatry, Kalpana Chawla Government Medical College and Hospital, Karnal, Haryana.
Email: [2]1prashantsrivastava@gmail.com

Parenting, a wonderful and rewarding experience, is sometime accompanied by high levels of stress, because of the difficulties, frustrations, and challenges that parents face in everyday life. The coming of a child with autism brings unexpected demands and challenges to parents, for which they are often not prepared. Having a child with autism has life changing implications and long-lasting effects on the entire family. Many aspects of family life and dynamics are adversely affected and on the other hand a few aspects get strengthened. Parents of children with autism experience heightened anxiety, overburden and marginalization in society, sense of self blame, tiredness or exhaustion. For a few parents it may mean the loss of a job. Strategies of coping with stress and management of the burden of care giving both assumed a paramount significance in the enhancement of family life and in the child's ultimate integration within society. The present paper aims to know the stress and care giving burden of parents having children with autism. Professionals from different disciplines such as psychology, medicine and social work need to develop interventions which are based on empirical studies. This paper recommends the role of social work professionals towards mitigating the stress among parents of children with autism.

Keywords: Stress, care giving burden and autism

A Study the Burnout in Health Care Professionals Working in Govt. and Private Intuitions

Kaplu Sharma[1], Atul Kumar Rai[1]

[1]Medical Social Worker, Post Graduate Institute of Medical Education and Research, Chandigarh
Email: atul.sw2007@gmail.com

Introduction: Role of health care professionals in Health setup has been widely acknowledged throughout the globe. The work carried out by these health care professionals has been phenomenal. In health care professionals Career burnout has turned into a common phenomenon in recent times. The basic reason is that every profession is susceptible to exhaustion and mental strain. To deal effectively with this problem, people need to differentiate normal stress from more serious issues that cause career burnout and found to be poor coping strategies with these kinds of problems. Aim and objective: The aim of the present study is to assess the burnout in health care professionals working in Govt. & Private instutions. Methods: This study is carried out at the Chandigarh and Tri City. The study will be a cross sectional and the sample will be selected through purposive sampling technique. The sample will consist of 60 health care professionals those who are working in health setup. Sample will be selected as per the inclusion and exclusion criterion of the study. Written informed consent will be taken from the samples of either group before starting data collection. The socio-demographic sheet and Copenhagen Burnout Inventory to Problems Experience will be applied on the selected sample. Result & Conclusion: The results of the study will be discussed at the time of presentation.

Keywords: Health Care Professional's burnout

Social Work Intervention in Disability: A study

Khillare Dinesh Digambar

Research Scholar, Department of Social Work, School of Social Sciences, Central University of Himachal Pradesh, Dharamshala Email: dinesh189khillare@gmail.com

Disability is a social as well as human right issue. More than 70 million people are disabled in India and they are unable to have access to various resources. Consequently, such families and their offspring's are not getting adequate and basic nutritional and minerals which is essential component for overall growth and development. Hence the resultant effect may be shown in the effect of disability in any part of the body. The progressive schemes like Mid Day Meal scheme and Sarva Shiksha Abhiyan was initiated to promote education and with an objective so that nutritional requirements of the students can be fulfilled. But it is heartening that many such students are being deprived of such benefits. As once disability occurs to the body such individuals had to face many struggles in their lifetime which may be understood in limited job availability, dependence on others. Although the government sector had an access to jobs to such persons who are disabled, as government jobs are limited, most of the potential that such disabled persons are having goes unnoticed and thus they face the atrocities of unemployment in addition to physical problem that they are facing. The proposed study will try to analyze disabled people employment, jobs, social exclusion and social status. The researcher is trying to show social work intervention in the field of disability.

Keywords: Disability, social work intervention, social exclusion, and unemployment.

Social Work Practice in the Field of Disability

Komal Preet

BDS Intern, Adesh University, Bathinda, Punjab
Email: komalpreet386@gmail.com

Characteristics that we contemporarily define as disabilities have existed in the human population from earliest recorded history. At various times in history, disability has been viewed as a blessing from deity or the deities, a punishment for sin, or a medical problem. Social workers have worked with persons with disabilities from the inception of the profession, and in recent years, social work has begun to embrace the concept of disability as diversity and to treat disability as diversity and welcome disabled persons as fully participating members of the society. Social work has begun welcoming persons with disabilities as fully participating members of the society, including valuable members of the profession. Disability can be understood through a number of perspectives, including moral, medical or minority or social models. Each of these models has influenced the education of social work students and the strategies used by professionals working with persons with disabilities.

Keywords: Social Work Practice, Disability

Scope of Psychiatric Social Worker in Community Mental Health Program: Field Experience and Observation

Krishan Kumar[1], Deepalatha R[2]

[1]PGIMER, Chandigarh, [2]TISS, Mumbai
Email: krishan2056@gmail.com

Background: Community psychiatry is one of the streams of psychiatry and is currently in developing process. Indian community psychiatry policies and community mental health services are considered best in developing countries. But CMHPs are unable to achieve its said goal because of cultural disparities, over population, remote locations, very large and diverse country, lack of finance and lack of trained professionals. One more important cause is roles and scope of different professionals in community team was not understood. Dept. of Psychiatry PGIMER Chandigarh started a rural community based mental health program. The program is different from traditional way of community psychiatry clinics. A village called Nandpur Kalour in Fatehgarh Sahib (Punjab) was chosen and a team of two social worker, senior resident and junior resident designated to visit village once in week. This community program gave insight to this paper. Aim and Objectives: To emphasis on scope of Psychiatric Social Worker (PSWs) in community mental health services. Methodology: Present paper is based on working experience, discussions and observation in community psychiatry field. Results: During field work we were enlightened with the fact that social issues like caste system, gender disparities, awareness, cultural legitimacy, language, education, occupation, Stigma etc. are main hurdle in CMHPs. Conclusion: So the most of difficulties are social in nature, therefore scope of PSWs in CMHPs is important and they must be utilized at fullest.

Keywords: Psychiatric Social Worker, Community Mental Health Programme and Experience

Social Work Intervention- Relocation and Rehabilitation of Without attendant/ Unknown/ Destitute patients in Department of Emergency Medicine at All India Institute of Medical Sciences Delhi

Leema[1], B.R.Shekhar[2], A.K.Chaurasiya1 , Abhishek[1], Aftab1,Md. Shahid1, Vivek[1]

[1]MSSO GRADE-II (Medical Social Welfare Unit Main Hospital RAK OPD), AIIMS, Delhi
[2]Chief MSSO, AIIMS, Delhi. Email: leemaroy18@gmail.com

The Social worker's aim is to improve and facilitate the working of society & its environment, and develop social institute through human relationships. Though Social Workers in Emergency uphold a protocol during intervention in the lives of without attendant/ Unknown/ destitute patients; still their core intention is to improve the social life of indigent patients and increasing their solidarity in society with human cooperation. 134 without attendant/ Unknown/ destitute patients received Social Intervention by Medical Social Service Officers in Emergency during the period of April 2017 and January 2018 through the coordination with the team of treating medical practitioners & police personnel. Different protocols are followed for Medico Legal Cases (MLC) and Non-Medico Legal Cases. Out of 134 patients, more than 60% were registered as MLC. 76% patients were Male and almost one third of total patients were brought by their relatives, good Samaritans, security guards of the institute or referred from Trauma Centre, AIIMS to the casualty. Maximum number of patients were conscious and oriented, however only 40% of them were finally received by their relatives/friends. More than 80% of the total patients were relocated from Emergency. They were shifted either to different wards for further treatment or relocated to their home addresses, working places or handed over to their relatives. Few of them left on their own. Almost 11% without attendant/ Unknown/ destitute patients were rehabilitated in shelter homes in Delhi & NCR. We found a significant correlation in relocation of patients and their relatives. Whereas as the correlation between locating the relatives and sex of the patients were insignificant. Our study concludes that social work intervention for without attendant/ Unknown/ destitute patients of emergency have enhanced their well being by providing them a solution for problems in human relationship with social changes.

Keywords: Social Work, Relocation and Rehabilitation, Destitute patients, AIIMS Delhi

Life Satisfaction among the Spouses of Individuals with Alcohol Dependence Syndrome as Compared with Normal Control

Mayank Singh[1], Jai Shanker Patel[2], Manisha Kiran[3]

[1]M.Phil Scholar, [2]Ph.D Scholar, [3]Associate Professor and Head,
Department of Psychiatric Social Work, RINPAS, Ranchi, Jharkhand Email: mayanksinghrak@gmail.com

Background: Alcoholism is like a disease which does not only affect the individual but the whole family. Studies reveal that spouses' well being and way of life is influenced by their partner's alcohol problems. Spouses of individual with alcohol dependence syndrome are affected on many different levels. Several studies have shown that spouses of individual with alcohol dependence syndrome often present significant rates of mental and physical problems, communication problems, low social activity and poor marital satisfaction. The spouses develop ways of dealing with the concomitant stress, a coping behavior which seems to be rather uniform even though spouses of individual with alcohol dependence syndrome are, of course a heterogeneous group with varying backgrounds. The alcoholism causes stress in the relationship, and being exposed to this kind of stress is highly detrimental. Alcohol misuse affects couples' relationships in a variety of negative ways, e.g. increased conflict, communication problems, poor sexual relations and domestic violence. This study was planned to assess the life satisfaction of spouses of these individuals. Objective: To examine life satisfaction among the spouses of individuals with alcohol dependence syndrome as compared with normal control and to compare the differences in both the groups. Methodology: The study sample will be consisted of 60 divided into following two groups will be included from Ranchi Institute of Neuro- Psychiatry & Allied Science, Ranchi. Purposive sampling technique will be used for the selection of sample. Age, education and income of family will be matched in the both groups. Socio demographic information, life satisfaction for spouses of individuals with alcohol dependence syndrome and Healthy Controls, will be used for the data collection. Data collected will be analyzed using Statistical Package for Social Sciences (SPSS- 16 version). Results and Conclusion: Results and Implications will be discussed during the time of presentation.

Keywords: Life Control, Alcohol Dependence Syndrome.

Burden of Care and coping in care givers among People with Bipolar Affective Disorder

Menka[1], **Neetu Sheokand**[2], **Rakesh Kumar**[3] **& Pradeep Kumar4**

[1]Psychiatric Social Worker (DMHP), Civil Hospital Rohtak,
[2]M.Phil, Psychiatric Social Work. Deptment of Psychiatry, PTBD Sharma, UHS, Rohtak.
[3]Psychiatric Social Worker (DMHP), Civil Hospital Fetehabad.
[4]Consultant, Psychiatric Social Work, State Institute of Mental Health, PD,
B.D. Sharma University of Health Sciences, Rohtak, Haryana.
Email: menkadec@gmail.com

Backgound: Bipolar Affective Disorder (once commonly known as manic depression or manic depressive illness) is one of the most common, severe and persistent psychiatric illnesses. It is a disorder that causes unusual shifts in mood, energy, activity level and the ability to carry out day to day task. Symptoms of bipolar disorder are severe. Aims and objectives: The aim of the study was to determine the care givers burden of the person with Bipolar Affective Disorder. Methodology: The study was descriptive. Caregivers of 30 individuals diagnosed with Bipolar Affective Disorder admitted in the Department of Psychiatry, PGIMS, Rohtak were selected purposively, those who fulfilled the inclusion and exclusion criteria Tools: Socio-demographic & clinical Performa, The global assessment of functioning by Endicott, Spitzer and Fleiss (1976), Copying check list by Nehra et al (2002) and Family burden interview schedule developed by Pai S, Kapur RL (1981) were applied. Statistical Analysis: Appropriate analysis was carried out using Statistical Package for social sciences (16.0). Results and conclusion: The global burden was high among most of the participants and they used different coping styles to deal with. There was moderate level dysfunction among patients who participated for the study. It was found that there was significant correlation among total family burden and total coping score. Apart from total coping, family burden had significant relationship with the avoidance style of coping.

Keywords: Burden, Coping, Caregiver and Bipolar Disorder

Gender difference in family attitude and Family burden people living with schizophrenia

Monika[1], **Bhupendra Singh**[2]

[1]Scholar M. Phil, [2]Assistant Professor, Department of Psychiatric Social Work, Institute of Mental Health,
Pt. B.D. Sharma University of Health Sciences, Rohtak.
Email: 33bhupendrasingh@gmail.com

Family members and their difficulties are the focused area of research in developed countries. Schizophrenia is a clinical syndrome of variable, but profoundly disruptive psychopathology that involves cognition, emotion, perception, and other aspect of behavior. It is commonly known as functional psychosis. It is a chronic illness which affects the patient and the family in all functionalities. It impairs quality of life such as employment, marriage, and parenthood etc. Aim: To assess Gender difference in family attitude and social support among people living with schizophrenia Methods: On the basis of purposive sampling technique 30 patients living with schizophrenia will be selected from OPD of department of Psychiatry, Institute of Mental Health Pt. BD Sharma University of Health Sciences Rohtak. With the written consent caregiver of patients will be selected and family attitude questionnaire and family burden will be administered. Result: High Expressed was found towards female patients and similarly high burden was reported by caregivers in comparison to their male counterparts.

Keywords: Attitude, family, social support, schizophrenia.

Organ Procurement and Transplantation: Social Work Interventions in Hospital Settings

Mukesh Kumar

Medical Social Service Officer, AIIMS, New Delhi
Email: kmukesh72@gmail.com

Organ transplantation is a viable option of treatment for the patients whose organ functioning is severely compromised due to terminal illness requiring urgent replacement. Organs for transplantation can either be procured from living related and unrelated donors or deceased donors who, while alive, had expressed their wish to donate organs after death or whose family members are willing to donate their organs after the demise. The success of transplantation has not only offered opportunities for many patients to live a longer and quality life but also raised several problems. There is an acute shortage of human organs which may be attributed to many factors such as lack of awareness about organ donation, lack of adequate guidelines and procedures to harvest organs in hospitals, ignorance and resistance in hospital staff to identify potential donors and non-acceptance of brain stem death as death among general public. The expenditure incurred on transplant surgery and life-long medications is quite high. During transplantation process donors, recipients and their families often undergo various psycho-social stressors which may disrupt their functioning. Professional social workers are experts in rapport formation, psycho-social assessment, problem solving, crisis intervention, counseling, empathy, awareness campaigns, resource mobilization etc. which can effectively be utilized in organ procurement and meeting the needs of donors, recipients and their families.

Keywords: Organ Procurement, Transplantation, Social Work and Hospital Settings

Sex Education of Children and Adolescents with Mental Illness

Nandini Sharma

M. Phil Clinical Psychology (1st year), Amity University, Lucknow. Email: nandini14sharma@gmail.com

Sex education is a program aiming to bring awareness about issues relating to human sexuality, which includes human sexual anatomy, sexual activities, sexual reproduction, age of consent, reproductive health, safe sex, reproductive rights, birth control and sexual abstinence. Sexual health is considered to be a state of physical, emotional, mental, and social well-being in relation to sexuality and not merely the absence of disease, dysfunction or infirmity (WHO, 2006). Sexual awareness is essential for persons with mental illness. A review of literature indicates that lack of knowledge about sexual health and sexual practices may make persons with mental illness more prone to inappropriate sexual practices as well as they are at a greater risk of sexual abuse. The current paper aims to sensitize towards the importance of sexual education for children and adolescents with mental illness. The review also explores the issues of feasibility and acceptability of sex education for children and adolescents with mental illness in the Indian context. This is done on the basis of findings from literature from India and other countries.

Keywords: Sex education, Mental Illness, Children, Adolescents

Psychiatric Social Worker Services in Drug De-Addiction Centre

Neetu Rani

Psychiatric Social Worker, Drug De-addiction and Treatment Centre, PGIMER, Chandigarh.
Email: neetupsw@gmail.com

The Drug De-Addiction Centre at PGIMER Chandigarh started functioning in the year 1978. Apart from providing quality performance services to the needy, the centre is currently a teaching, training and research centre. Here persons with substance use disorder are given professional services by a team of psychiatrists, psychiatric social workers, clinical psychologists and psychiatric nurses. In this poster, the author is trying to provide an outline of Drug De-Addiction Centre at PGIMER, the multi furious services rendered, here with a special emphasize on the roles of psychiatric social workers at In-Patient, Out-Patient and community levels.

Keywords: Drug De-addiction and Treatment Centre, Psychiatric Social Worker

Community Based Rehabilitation and Person with Disability: An Emerging Issue in India

Neetu[1], Meneka[2], Rakesh Kumar[3], Pradeep Kumar[4]

[1] M.Phil, Psychiatric Social Work. Department of Psychiatry, PTBD,Sharma,UHS ,Rohtak.
[2] Psychiatric Social Worker (DMHP), Civil Hospital, Rohtak
[3] M.Phil, Psychiatric Social Work, Psychiatric Social Worker, Civil Hospital Fatehabad,
[4]Consultant, Psychiatric Social Work, State Institute of Mental Health,
PD, B.D.Sharma University of Health Sciences, Rohtak. Email: sheokandneetu@gmail.com

Background: Community-based Rehabilitation (CBR) is a strategy within general community development, for the rehabilitation, equalization of opportunities and social inclusion of all people with disabilities. Disability is not just a health problem. It is a complex phenomenon, reflecting the interaction between features of a person's body and features of the society in which he or she lives. Aims: To aware and sensitize the Divyangjan, their care givers and various stoke holders towards community based rehabilitation for person with disability. Overcoming the difficulties faced by people with disabilities requires interventions to remove environmental and social barriers. Right of Person with Disability Act 2016 replaces the Persons with Disabilities Act, 1995. Methodology: Literature search of both electronic databases including PubMed and manual searches Conclusion: This Act not only enhances the Rights and Entitlements of Divyangjan but also provide effective mechanism for ensuring their empowerment and true inclusion into the Society in a satisfactory manner. CBR is an effective strategy for increasing community level activity for equalization of opportunities for people with disabilities by including them in programmes focused on human rights, poverty reduction and inclusion.

Keywords: Disability, Rehabilitation, Social Inclusion.

Organ Donation: A Qualitative Study Exploring the Reasons Behind Living Organ Donation

Nishtha Mishra[1], Muthusamy Sivakami [2]

[1]Nishtha Mishra, Research Scholar, School of Social Work, Tata Institute of Social Sciences, Mumbai.
[2]MuthusamySivakami, Professor, Centre for Health and Social Sciences, School of Health Systems Studies, Tata Institute of Social Sciences, Mumbai. Email: nishtha.mishra2016@tiss.edu

Organ transplantation is a medical treatment for the end stage organ failure diseases such as liver, heart and kidney disease. The rapid advancement in transplant process has become a life-saving procedure for the patients suffering from chronic illness. Available data on Indian Transplant Registry reflects that the status of organ donation in India is quite shocking. Almost 1.5 lakh people are in need of a kidney, however, only 3,000 of them receives. Annual liver transplant requirement is 25,000 however 800 out of them receives a liver. Among the registered member for cadaver organ, 90% of them die without getting an organ. For fulfilling the requirement of organs and shortage of cadaver organs has contributed in promoting living organ donation. Thus, it is important to understand the living organ donation with the perspective of those who have donated they're while being alive. The objective of present study was to explore the reasons behind organ donation. A qualitative methodology with a narrative approach focusing on the stories narrated by the individual related to their experiences was conducted in Rajasthan state at the community level. Snowball sampling was used for collecting data and a total of 17 participants were included in the study. The data was collected through in-depth interviews with the help of in-depth interview guide prepared by the researcher. In the present study, four reasons were stated by the participants for donating an organ. Relationship status, social role, voluntarism and various circumstances such as helplessness of the family and recipient's health condition were some of the reason for donating an organ. The data does not find any organ donation happened on a monetary basis. All the participants of the study were having blood relation and the donation happened for saving the life of the recipient. There was no difference found in the familial, social and economic levels among the participants stating the reason based on circumstances. But the gender-based differences can be observed in the reasons such as relationship status and social role. The present study reveals that reasons of donating organ vary from individual to individual. These reasons are an influential factor in decision making. The reasons are the results of situational based aspect which the donor had experienced throughout the illness and suffering of the recipient as a family member or a caregiver. The exploration of the reasons behind organ donation reflects the circumstances in which Indian people donate their organs while being alive. It also reflects the gap in the need of cadaver organ which indirectly promoting living organ donation in India.

Keywords: Living organ donation, Relationship Status, Social Role, Voluntarism, Gender disparity.

Role of Medical Social Worker in Neuro-Psychiatric Hospital

Pappu Rajak

Medical Social Worker (MSW), Institute of Human Behavior Allied Science (IHBAS) Delhi
Email: rajakihbas@gmail.com

Medical social worker (MSW) play important role in Hospital setting. They play vital role in patient care services on day to day basis in both out patient department (O.P.D.) as well as in Patient department (I.P.D.). The establishment of social work school led to the beginning of professionalization of social work in India. The first Medical Social worker was appointed in 1946 in J.J Hospital, Bombay. MSW work as a team member in the multidisciplinary/Hospital team consisting doctors,(Neurologist, Psychiatrist, Neurosurgery.) nursing and paramedical staff.MSW improve resources for patients and their caregivers and liaison with the hospital team, non government organization, and other related agencies for rehabilitation of patients. Medical Social Worker help in arranging financial support, for carrying out patients' treatment wherever needed from Governmental or Non-governmental organizations. They deal with income assessment and background assessment for the poor socio-economic patients, and coordinate in the area of discharge planning, assist with the doctor in the patients discharge. MSW also suggest ways to the patient and his family for reduction burden on the families, MSW counsel patients and their families regarding how to deal with symptoms and treatment effectively. They give intervention for psycho social need and dealing of interpersonal problems. MSW deals with public grievances referral, public relation, court visit referrals with follow-up, coordination for various awareness programmes in different clinical disciplines, and facilitate patient and their families to get different welfare scheme of Govt.

Keywords: Role, MSW, Neuro-Psychiatric Hospital

Level of Awareness about Blood Donation in Rural & Urban Community: A Comparative Study

Pardeep Kumar, Atul Kumar Rai

Medical Social Worker, PGIMER, Chandigarh Email: atul.sw2007@gmail.com

Introduction: Blood donation is a boon to medical industry as it has helped in saving the. There is a great need for treatment. There is no age limit for blood donation. A patient's medical history is more important than the age of the donor. If a patient has a normal functioning and is in good health, then blood donation is certainly an option. Newborns as well as senior citizens have been blood donors.. Aim and objective: To assess Level of Awareness and compare about blood donation in Rural as compare with urban community. Methods: This study is carried out at the Chandigarh and near Tri City. The study will be a cross sectional and the sample will be selected through purposive sampling technique. The sample will consist of 60 participants belongs to rural & urban area. Sample will be selected as per the inclusion and exclusion criterion of the study. Written informed consent will be taken from the samples of either group before starting data collection. The socio-demographic sheet and semi structured Performa will be applied on the selected sample. Result & Conclusion: The results of the study will be discussed at the time of presentation

Keywords: Blood Donation etc.

Social Work Interventions in Surgical Gastroenterology patients

R.Srividhya[1], Biju Pottakkat[2], V. Chitraleka[3]

[1]Medical Social Worker, MSS WING, [2]Additional Professor and Head, Dept of SGE,
[3]Social Service Officer, MSS Wing, JIPMER. Email: ksrividhya@gmail.com

Department of Surgical Gastroenterology was established in 2010 at Super speciality JIPMER. It provides care for patients with a continuum of the complex surgical problems in GI tract. Role of social work interventions in liver transplant patient, department of surgical gastroenterology is tested as a case study. Medical Social Worker acts as an intermediate link between the medical team and the patient. The patients, care givers and family members are assisted to cope with problems resultant of illness and treatment through comprehensive psycho social support and care needed for focused intervention and services. The services include pre and post-operative counseling, health education, treatment adherence, individual counseling, couple and family counseling, group therapy, palliative support, crisis intervention, financial assistance, guidance on availing community resources and referrals. The patients are regularly consulted in the outpatient department. Special outpatient clinics include weekly Liver clinic and Obesity clinic. Special programs of the department are HPB and Liver Transplant surgery, Advanced Laparoscopic GI surgery, State of art Robotic surgery, Bariatric and Metabolic surgery. The inpatient ward has 20 beds, intensive care unit has 6 beds, liver transplant intensive care unit has 6 beds, and special wards are provided with counseling and support. Assessments and Interventions are done systematically and are being documented. Frequent surveys are conducted to assess the patient satisfaction to the care delivery system and also orientation given to master of social work students of various universities.

Keywords: Social Work Interventions, Surgical Gastroenterology

Health Risk and Vulnerability of the People Working in the Marble Processing Units in Kishangarh, Ajmer district, Rajasthan

Rajeev M.M

Assistant Professor, Department of Social Work,
School of Social Sciences, Central University of Rajasthan Email- rajeevmm@curaj.ac.in

India is the biggest country in the production of marble and Rajasthan has been ranked first in marble mining. In Asia, Kishangarh block in Ajmer (India) has the biggest market in the world and there are about 1100 marble processing units all over the Rajasthan. Sharma (2007) analyzed that the mineworkers have to work there every day where dangerous mineral dust - laden air occurs which cause many lung diseases such as silicosis, tuberculosis (TB), tuberculosis and asthma. Large amounts in concentrations of dust can be a health hazard, exacerbating respiratory disorders such as asthma and irritating the lungs and bronchial passages. The current study is an attempt to understand and analyze the nature of health risks and vulnerability of the workers in the marble processing centers in Kishangarh block, Ajmer district. Secondly, the study is intended to find out the general health related issues of working people in the marble industry. Thirdly, the study is tried to make an attempt to understand the psychosocial condition of working people in the Marble Industry. Furthermore, the study also will look in to the possibilities of an intervention from the part of Department of Social Work, Central University of Rajasthan by facilitating sensitization, health care development activities with the support of multiple stakeholders. Descriptive research design was adopted for the study and the researcher used quantitative method for collecting the data. The study universe is working people in the marble industries of area Kishangarh Dis. Ajmer. The primary data was collected from the respondents from the locations such as Haramara, Bhojiyawas, Paloda, Tiloniya, Patan and Banjaraki and Dhani. The sample size is 100 including both men and women in the age group between 14 to 60 Apart from this, FGD's were conducted to get more information. The findings imply that there is an urgent need of addressing the various health concerns of the people working in the marble processing industries.

Keywords: Marble mining, descriptive research design, silicosis, FGD's

Family Stress and Dyadic Adjustment among Parents of Children with Intellectual Disability and Functional Psychosis: A Comparative Study

Raja Upadhyay[1], Jagritee Singh[2], S. H. Nizamie[3], N. K. Singh[4]

[1]Psychiatric Social Worker, District Mental Health Unit, Sadar Hospital, Bhabhua, Kaimur, Bihar
[2]Ph. D Scholar, Department of Social Work, Jamia Millia Islamia, New Delhi.
[3]Professor of Psychiatry (Rtd.) Central Institute of Psychiatry, Ranchi
[4]P.S.W., Department of Psychiatric Social Work, Central Institute of Psychiatry, Ranchi.
Email:rajaup92@gmail.com

Introduction: Being a parent can be both rewarding and challenging, even for parents of children without disabilities. The expense and time it takes to raise a child is compounded when a child has a disability. Children with developmental and/or intellectual disabilities and fuctional psychosis may require additional time and expense to provide independent living and rehabilitative services. The stress of having a child with a developmental and/or intellectual disability and fubctional psychosis can take a toll on parents and cause relationship stress. Aim & Objective: The purpose of this study was to assess and compare the family stress and dyadic relationship among parent of children with intellectual disability and functional psychosis. Participants and Methods: This study was a cross-sectional hospital based study. The study samples were selected through purposive sampling technique. The sample size was 40 parents among which 20 parents of children and adolescent with intellectual disability and 20 parents of children and adolescent with functional psychosis taken from Erna Hoch Child and Adolescent Psychiatry Unit and Charak Outpatient Department, of the Central Institute of Psychiatry, Kanke, Ranchi. Depression Anxiety and Stress Scale and Dyadic Adjustment scale was used for the data collection. Data were analyzed by Statistical Package for Social Sciences (SPSS-21 version). Results: Findings indicated no significant group differences in rating scale. However trend was seen in the sub domain of stress (.069) in Depression, anxiety and stress scale. In Spearman correlation test positive correlation were found in sub domains of depression, Anxiety and stress and dyadic adjustment scale, between depression and affectional relationship and with depression and satisfaction in the parents of children with intellectual disability. Conclusion: Both groups of parents are suffering from same kind of stress so Government and NGO's should focus on services for parents or caregivers of intellectually disabled and functional psychotic children and adolescents such as counseling centres, parents support groups, free medical treatment, in each and every tertiary treatment centres in our country.

Keywords: Family Stress, Dyadic Adjustment, Psychosis and Intellectual Disability

Challenges for Social Work Education in India: Voices of Social Work Students

Rajendra Baikady[1] Channaveer R.M[1] , Cheng Shengli[2]

[1]Department of Social Work, Central University of Karnataka, India,

[2]Department of Social Work, ShangDong, China Email: rajendrabaikady@yahoo.com

Social Work as an academic discipline in India has seen almost eight decades of its existence. The first professional social work training course was started in 1936 much earlier than India got its independence. In the initial years the training and teaching was much on labour welfare and other welfare related issues. Gradually the focus of social work shifted from nonprofessional support to professional support and social work academia made an effort to establish its own academic credentials. As result more and more educational institutions started offering courses both at graduate and post graduate levels. To date there are more than 600 schools and departments of social work offering social work education at different levels. Starting from one school offering the course and presently a web of institutions involved in academic engagement, social work education in India experienced many ups and downs through its development. Even after eighty years of education and practice social work in India is not well recognized, it doesn't have an accrediting body and Professional recognition with in the country. This paper gives voice to social work students on some of the challenges, including curriculum, pedagogy, recognition of the profession, and practicum. The paper is based on the interviews with, students from five universities in India, and includes concrete recommendations for improving the professional training of social work students.

Challenges for Social Work Education in India: Voices of Social Work Educators

Rajendra Baikady[1] Channaveer R.M[1] , Cheng Shengli[2]

[1]Department of Social Work, Central University of Karnataka, India,

[2]Department of Social Work, ShangDong, China Email: rajendrabaikady@yahoo.com

This article presents the social work educators perception on challenges for social work education in India. Literature on social work education including curriculum, practice and pedagogy provided the framework for the study. The study reported on the results of qualitative interviews conducted to social work educators (n= 33) across five schools of social work in New Delhi, Mumbai and Kolkata in India. The study finds that there are four major challenges for social work education in India: (i) Problem of definition; (ii) lack of regulatory framework and diversity among the schools; (iii) lack of professional identity

Keywords: Social Work Education, Curriculum, Pedagogy, Field practicum

Level of Determination and Dependence among person with Alcohol Dependence

Rakesh Kumar [1], Neetu Sheokand [2], Menka [3], Pradeep Kumar [4]

[1]M.Phil, Psychiatric Social Work, Psychiatric Social Worker, Civil Hospital Fatehabad,
[2]M.Phil, Psychiatric Social Work. Department of Psychiatry, PTBD,Sharma,UHS ,Rohtak.
[3]Psychiatric Social Worker (DMHP), Civil Hospital, Rohtak
[4]Consultant, Psychiatric Social Work, State Institute of Mental Health,
PD, B.D.Sharma University of Health Sciences, Rohtak. Email: rakesh.mathur767@gmail.com

Background: The problem of excessive alcohol consumption is a major cause of public health concern in most countries in the word today. Heavy consumption, which involves far more than dependence, can cause untold misery to the individual, who is usually affected by other physical, psychological and social disabilities as well. Alcohol is one of the leading causes of the death and disability globally. About two billion people worldwide consume alcoholic beverage and one third is likely to have one or more diagnosable alcohol use disorders. Aim: The current study aimed to determine the Severity of Dependence and level of motivation among individuals with Alcohol Dependence Syndrome. Methodology: Purposive sampling techniques were used having 50 individuals diagnosed with Alcohol Dependence Syndrome from the Drug de-addiction center, PGIMS, Rohtak. Tools: Socio-demographic & clinical Performa, Alcohol dependence scale, Michigan alcohol screening test, Readiness to change questionnaire were applied. Statistics: Appropriate analysis was done using Statistical Package for Social Sciences-version.16.Results and conclusion: Maximum respondents had intermediate to substantial level of dependency. And almost all the samples were "problem drinkers". Half the patients participated in the study were in the pre contemplation stage of motivation.

Keyword: Determination, Dependence and Alcohol Dependence

Social Work Practice in Open Defecation Free Movement: A Special Reference to Rural District of North India

Ravindra Khaiwal[1], Sanjeev Kumar[2]

[1]Additional Professor, [2]Medical Social Worker,
Department of Community Medicine, School of Public Health, PGIMER Chandigarh.
Email: sanjeevsingla89@gmail.com

Under the Swachh Bharat Mission (SBM) or clean India movement, India would become open defecation-free by October 2019. It was an ambitious target considering that 524 million Indians (till June 2017) defecate in the open every day, according to the UN figures. The last three consecutive years around 260 districts have been declared open defecation free. But the various studies show that ODF is not maintained properly. Still, the number of people defecated openly even after the toilet construction at their household level. Studies after studies have pointed out that ending open defecation is not just about building toilets but changing the behavior of people and inspiring them to use toilets According to expenditure details for FY 17-18 available on the government SBM portal, the total available fund with states in terms of Centre's share was Rs 10678.49 crore, out of which, Rs 200.70 crore was spent on IEC activities, which is only 1.87 percent of the total fund. So states should spend more on behavioral change aspect of the SBM. They should adopt the community led total Sanitation (CLTS) which is based on community participation and motivation. The professional social workers have particular skills and techniques which are very useful for CLTS. The present article deals with applied skills and techniques of social workers which are used for first ODF declared district of Fatehgarh Sahib of Punjab.

Keywords: Social work practice, open defecation free movement and North India

Depression, Anxiety and Stress among Alcohol Dependence patients

Reena[1], Sunila[2], Bhupendra Singh[3]

[1]M.Phil. scholar Psychiatric Social Work, [2]Assistant Professor, [3]Assistant Professor PSW
Institute of Mental Health, Pt. B. D. Sharma University of Health Sciences, Rohtak, Haryana
Email: reenaverma247@gmail.com

Introduction: Depression, anxiety and stress are the very common problem among the Alcohol dependents. The present study was conducted to assess the differences between Alcohol dependents and normal controls in the area of Depression, Anxiety and Stress. Aim: Aim of the present study is to assess the Depression, Anxiety and Stress among alcohol dependent patients. Methods: 30 male alcohol dependent subjects age range between 18-50 selected on the basis of purposive sampling from the State Drug De-addiction and Training Centre, Institute of Mental Health, Pt. B.D. Sharma UHS Rohtak. Inform consent will be sought from the participants, self-structured socio demographic data sheet will be filled followed by DASS 21 Hindi Version. Result: Depression Anxiety and Stress are associated with alcohol dependence. Findings also suggest that high score of depression is associated with higher level of anxiety and stress.

Keywords: Depression, Anxiety, Stress, Alcohol Dependence

Corporate Social Responsibility- An Instrument for Promoting Supportable Healthcare Practices

Rifat Anjum

Doctoral Scholar, Department of Social Work, Jamia Millia Islamia, New Delhi
Email: rifatkhursheed@gmail.com

Health is a crucial aspect of human development. With the rapid increase in every industry, healthcare industry is also growing at a tremendous pace. Increase in native demands, upsurge in advanced healthcare services, incursion of medical tourism and rising expenditure by both public and private players. Although, India has advanced its boundaries in healthcare sector still vast ambit of population till date have minimal access to proper healthcare facilities. CSR involves strategic planning and proper implementation of activities for the welfare and development of underserved people. CSR can act as a resource which paves way for considering the persistent problems that are cropping in the health setting. The amenities provided by hospitals do not reach out to the masses that lack accessibility to the available facilities. CSR will help the healthcare sector to elaborate on social issues that could serve to improve their images and enhance the stakeholder engagement by making their performance indicators available to public. The objective of the paper includes elucidating the present status of healthcare industry, the challenges healthcare setting is facing especially with reference to its role in the larger society and elaborating on the role of CSR in enriching healthcare amenities. Secondary sources of data in the form of literature were used to give a theoretical role of CSR in healthcare industry. The paper concludes by recommending the need for various industries to collaborate and work on the same tangent to achieve the goal that CSR is set to achieve.

Keywords: Corporate Social responsibility, Promotion and Health Care Practice

Transactional Analysis in Nursing as a Profession

Rohini Thapar[1], Navneet Nancy[2]

[1]Assistant Professor, Dept. of Psychology, D.A.V. College, Chandigarh
[2]Research Scholar, Dept. of Psychology, Panjab University, Chandigarh
Email: n09.nancy@gmail.com

Transactional analysis is a theory of human personality and social behavior. It is a comprehensive system of psychotherapy founded in late 1950's by Eric Berne. Lately, organizational psychologists are waking up to the value of transactional analysis as a valuable HR tool, giving them an insight into various interpersonal transactional styles in various professions. Nursing as a profession has always been characterized as a nurturing, care giving and comfort providing job, which can emerge as a very taxing and stressful profession in return (Luthans, 2005). The myriad role that nurses play requires certain interpersonal tacts and styles which are very typical demands of their job role. But their individual personalities and dispositions cannot be ignored. Hence, an attempt is being made in the present study to analyze different transactional styles being adopted by female nursing professionals, along with their back up styles and also the role of their marital status on how they deal with their patients. For this purpose, a sample of 120 female nurses, 60 married and 60 unmarried, falling in the age range of 25-40 years, working in various private and government hospitals of Chandigarh was taken and the differences between the two groups were calculated using t test. Findings and implications will be discussed.

Keywords: Nurses, Transactional analysis, transactional styles, nurse-patient interaction

Effect of Emotional Maturity on Mental Health

Ruchi Chauhan

Research Scholar, Jain Vishva Bharti Insititue, Landnun, Rajasthan
Email: ruchisingh9220@gmail.com

The Present Paper discussed on primarily conducted to find the Correlation between mental Health and Emotional Maturity. There is extensive research linking healthy, Social and emotional development to effective parenting. Emotional Maturity is the Product of interaction between many factors of society, it also helps to contain the growth of adolescent's development. The Concept of Maturity means Balanced Personality. But as we Knew Emotional Pressure increasing day by day at adolescent age. A man who is emotionally stable will have better adjustment with others and she/he will have more satisfaction. Maturity is a tool for Promoting student's mental health and personality. In same way Adolescents is transitional period and it is a span Between Childhood & Adulthood. According to W.H.O (1997) it starts about from ten years of age and continues through nineteen years.

Keywords: Emotional Maturity, Adolescent, Mental Health

Social Worker in Hospital: A Bridge between Patient and Administration for Smooth Functioning of Services in Hospital

S.K Srivastava

Medical Social Service Officer, SGPGIMS, Lucknow
Email: pankajs82@yahoo.co.in

Medical social worker works with patients and their families in need of psychosocial intervention and get involved in treatment plan of patients. Interventions may include connecting patients and families to useful resources and supports in hospital and community. On other hand medical social worker have some expectation from administration to improve smooth functioning of services in hospital. This presentation is regarding experience of medical social worker in hospital.

Keywords: Hospital, Medical Social Worker

Role Perception and Role Performance of Professional Social Workers in Hospital Settings

Shashi Kant Srivastava[1], Bijendra Pradhan[2]

[1]Research Scholar, [2]Head,
Department of Social Work, Jain Vishva Bharati Institute, Ladnun, Rajasthan,
Email: getkantshashi@gmail.com

The Medical Council of India in its Report (1973) recommended appointment of at least 6 Medical Social Workers in the Medical settings having 100 admissions. Despite such a mandatory direction, those responsible for providing medical are- the planners, the Governments at the Centre and in different states, and medical care institutions providing medical care of different varieties, have shown their utter indifference towards utilization of the pivotal role that Professional Social Worker plays in the fuller recovery of the patients of various types. This could be due to a variety of reasons. While the qualifications, duties and functions of

Doctors and Para-medical staff are very well defined by the governments and other stakeholders but the role of the Professional Social Workers as well as their qualifications have not been professionally defined. In a state like Uttar Pradesh, anyone without proper training in medical social work and a Master's Degree in Social Work can be appointed a Professional Social Worker in its medical institutions. As a consequence, what these "Professional Social Workers" have ended up in doing can at best be generally termed as Public Relations work. By any yardstick, it is not what has been defined as Professional Social Work. This paper attempts to explore the role perception and role performance of Professional Social Workers in Hospital settings especially in the light of apprehensions that usually their professional competence is not dealt with seriously and management has some other options of work assigned to them.

Keywords: Role Perception, Performance, Hospital

Family of a Person with Severe Mental Illness: Intervention, Issues and Challenges

Saswati Chakraborti[1], Jahanara M. Gajendragad[2]

[1]Psychiatric Social Worker, [2]Associate Professor and Head
Department of Psychiatric Social Work, Institute of Human Behaviour and Allied Sciences, Delhi.
Email: saswati146@rediffmail.com

As part of the shift toward a balanced mental health care system, there is growing recognition of the role of families as primary care givers in care of both in-patient and community. In India, families are generally deeply involved with their ill- relatives but their issues and particular needs have often been overlooked. It is very important to build a healthy link with family care givers and mental health professionals. Mental illness can be an extremely painful and traumatic experience for all of the family and have huge impact on a family's financial and emotional component. It can decrease the quality of life of the patient's family members as well as can increase social distance for the family involved in care giving. Coping mechanism for dealing with persons with mental illness also differ from one family to another family. The families want understanding of the illness, support and specific suggestions for coping with behavior of their ill relatives. Family intervention can delay and even prevent relapse of a relative with mental illness. It can improve the person's functioning as well as the well being of the family. Here, an attempt has been made to understand the issues of families having person with mental illness, challenges faced by them through a few case studies and also focused on some specific interventions which can help family in effective dealing and better care giving.

Keywords: Intervention, Issues, Severe Mental Illness

Socio-demographics and Social Participation of Disabled Women: An Exploration based upon Rehabilitation Centres of West Tripura

Subhasish Saha[1], Durba Deb[1], Haimanti Sarkar[1]

[1]Medical Social Worker, Department of Community Medicine,
Agartala Government Medical College, Kunjaban, Agartala, West Tripura.
Email: subha_sish2004@yahoo.co.in

Background: Women with disabilities are the most marginalized in Indian society. The problems of women with disabilities become very complex with other factors such as social stigma and poverty .This study was interested to concentrate on socio-demographic profile and to identify the status and social participation of women with special needs in Tripura. Materials and Methods: The study was undertaken among 360 numbers of disabled women selected by stratified random sampling method from different blocks of west Tripura. A semi-structured interviewer-administered questionnaire was used. Results: The study has brought out that the mean age was 37.3 years and SD = 13.8. A majority, 78.6%, of the women with disabilities did not participate in the social gatherings and functions held outside home. A majority 70% of the women with disabilities said that they faced discrimination compared to others in enjoying social status. Conclusion: The multi dimensional nature of poverty and social exclusion affecting disabled women. In order to fight social participation, it is necessary to design measures tackling all the aspects involved. It is necessary to fight discrimination faced by disabled people and their families in their daily lives, in order to tackle social participation.

Keywords: Socio-demographics, Social Participation, Disabled Women, West Tripura

A Success Story of Heart Patient: Role of Medical Social Worker in Multi-professional Health Care Team

Sudha Gupta[1], Asha Rani[1]

[1]Medical Social Worker, Dept. of Cardiology, PGIMER, Chandigarh
Email: ashafour@gmail.com

According to "The New England Journal of Medicine" 13.17 million people are affected with rheumatic heart disease in India and it remains the largest cardiac cause of morbidity and mortality in children, adolescents and young adults especially among low-middle income countries. RHD is generally a disease of poverty connected with poor sanitation & other social determinants of poor health. This article provides the reader with an understanding of the social worker's role with heart patient and as part of the interdisciplinary team. Case study was used to illustrate the key components of social work practice, including Social Care, Social Advocacy, Socio-economic Assessment, and Resource mobilization. This case study analysis was conducted during the month from April to June, 2017. Interview and Observation tool was used to analyze the case study. This case study explored that any poor child with congenital & acquired heart diseases with a very poor economic status can lead a normal life with the help of right time intervention of skilled professional social worker. The present result suggested that due to intervention done by social worker, patient could reach the resources available in the community to get financial assistance for his complete treatment. With regular connectivity with the patient & family members, a young boy could overcome his impairment due to the illness and after all the clinical interventions the patient is able to lead a normal and comfortable life so that so he is coming to PGIMER, Chandigarh for his follow up visits from a far of place alone. With our positive re assurance for economic independence he is going to join his school back very soon.

Keywords: Heart Patients, Medical Social Worker, Multiprofessional

Trauma care systems in India: An observational Study

Suruchi Sharma1 , Sushil K.Vimal1, Sh.Ziley Singh Vical1

1Community Medicine, AIIMS, NIHFW, New Delhi.
Email: suruchi1516@gmail.com

Trauma-care systems in India are at a nascent stage of development. Industrialized cities, rural towns and villages coexist, with variety of health care facilities and almost complete lack of organized trauma care. There is gross disparity between trauma services available in various parts of the country. Rural India has inefficient services for trauma care, due to the varied topography, financial constraints and lack of appropriate health infrastructure. There is no national lead agency to coordinate various components of a trauma system. No mechanism for accreditation of trauma centres and professionals exists. Education in trauma life-support skills has only recently become available. A nationwide survey encompassing various facilities has demonstrated significant deficiencies in current trauma systems. Although injury is a major public-health problem, the government, medical fraternity and the society are yet to recognize it as a growing challenge. Accelerated urbanization and industrialization have led to an alarming increase in the rate of accidental injuries, crime and violence in India. An unprecedented increase in the number of vehicles has outpaced the development of adequate roads and highways. It is well recognized that our health care system is not fully equipped to meet the challenge. In 2015, Academy of Traumatology (India) undertook a maiden study of trauma systems, regardless of their stage of development or geographical region. One hundred and forty-five institutions across the country, including university hospitals, other government, non-government and private hospitals in urban and rural areas of all states in India were invited to participate in the survey. The survey consisted of a comprehensive questionnaire concerning all major components of a trauma system. Fifty institutions participated in the survey. The overall data was fairly representative of urban and rural settings, private and public hospitals and facilities across all geographical regions of the country. The responses were analysed and the findings are included here under appropriate headings.

Keywords: Trauma care, India and Observational Study

Do male and female trauma patients receive the same pre hospital care?

Suruchi Sharma

AIIMS New Delhi Email: suruchi1516@gmail.com

Background: Trauma-related mortality can be lowered by efficient pre hospital care. Less is known about whether gender influences the pre hospital trauma care provided. The aim of this study was to explore gender-related differences in pre hospital trauma care of severely injured trauma patients, with a special focus on triage, transportation, and interventions. Methods: We performed a retrospective observational study based on local trauma registries and hospital and ambulance records. A total of 200 trauma patients (100 males and 100 females)?>?15 years of age with an Injury Severity Score (ISS) of?>?15 transported to emergency care hospitals in the area were included. Results: Male patients had a 2.75 higher odds ratio (95 % CI, 1.2-6.2) for receiving the highest pre hospital priority compared to females on controlling for injury mechanism and vital signs on scene. No significant difference between genders was detected regarding other aspects of the pre hospital care provided. Conclusion: This study indicated that pre hospital prioritization among severely injured late adolescent and adult trauma patients differs between genders. Knowledge of a more diffuse presentation of symptoms in female trauma patients despite severe injury may help to adapt and improve pre hospital trauma care for this group.

Keywords: Trauma, Pre Hospital Care, Observational Follow up and Delhi NCR

Mapping the Knowledge and Understanding of Menstrual Hygiene and Menstrual Health in Delhi

Suruchi Sharma, Mohd. Yaseen, Sushil K.Vimal

1Community Medicine, AIIMS, NIHFW, New Delhi. Email: suruchi1516@gmail.com

Objective: The study was aimed to find out perceptions and practices about menstruation among adolescent school girls in Delhi rural urban areas. Methodology: A cross-sectional study was done among two urban and two rural schools which were feasible and gave written permission. Total 371 adolescent girls who attained menarche were interviewed after obtaining written informed consent from their parents followed by focus group discussion (FGDs). Results: About one-third (34.5%) and 42.05% respondents respectively considered menstruation as a problem and impure state. Sanitary pads were used by 77% girls and 43% had habit of washing genitalia with soap and water during menses. 59% respondents practices social isolation during menses. FGDs revealed that girls follow many restrictions and customs and still waiting for better health. Conclusion: Study indicates the urgent need of health educational activities among the adolescent girls, their parents and teachers for improving menstrual hygiene and removing myths and misconception regarding menstruation.

Keywords: Adolescent girls, Menstrual hygiene, School based study

Mindfulness Based Cognitive Therapy for Depression and Generalized Anxiety Disorder: A Comparative Study

Sweta[1], Upendra Singh[2]

[1]HOD, Clinical Psychology, Nai Subah, Varanasi.
[2]Consultant Psychiatric Social Worker, DMHP Unit, Sasaram, Bihar.
Email: swetacip@gmail.com

Background: Mindfulness based cognitive therapy (MBCT) is the very recent advances in attempting to prevent relapses in depressive symptoms. Also MBCT has been showing its efficacy in the management of different psychiatric disorders like Substance abuse, stress management, social anxiety and so on. Aim: Thus the study aim at finding the efficacy of MBCT in managing symptoms of depression and generalized anxiety disorder. Methodology: Purposive sampling technique was used and

6 participants diagnosed with GAD and 16 participants diagnosed with moderate depression with somatic syndrome as per ICD-10, DCR were selected for the study. Module: Therapy was planned for a period of 14 weeks consisting of 25 sessions. Initial phase focused on psycho education and learning of breathing and scanning techniques. Middle phase emphasized upon cognitive approaches and mindfulness techniques. Result: It was found that MBCT had beneficial effect upon participants of both the groups but has a very good outcome over participants with depression. Conclusion: The study concludes that being mindful helps individual deal with day-to-day anxiety.

Keywords: Mindfulness, breathing, body scanning, cognition, non-judgment

Cancer Patients in Punjab: An Overview

Talwinder Kaur

Research Scholar, Department of Social work, Punjabi University, Patiala.
Email: dhillon.ruby@rediffmail.com

Cancer is a very serious disease in human life affecting a very high number of patients every day. The cancer patients face many problems with this disease. It is observed that the numbers of cancer patients are increasing day by day in Punjab. Many causes like pesticides, tobacco, alcohol, pollution and changing life style are responsible for this increase. The data shows that Muktsar district is having the highest number of cancer patients and Patiala district is having lowest number of cancer patients in Malwa region of Punjab. According to the Punjab Government's door to door campaign 2013, the Muktsar and Patiala districts are reported to have 136.3 and 86.8 cancer patients per lakh population. Government and Non-Government Organizations provide services through various schemes and programmes and try to cure and prevent the disease of cancer, but even after these steps the cancer incidence is ever increasing. The cancer in this area has affected larger number of families in more than one ways. Therefore, in the backdrop of the seriousness of this problem, research would be conducted to explore the over-all situation of the patients besides looking into the welfare initiatives of the Government and the other Non-Government Organizations in that area. In this context, the main aim of the paper is cancer patients in Punjab an overview.

Keywords: Cancer Patients and Overview

Perceived Burden: A Comparative Gender Based Study among Intellectual Disabled at Sasaram

Upendra Singh[1], Sweta[2], V.K.Singh[3], R.K.Singh[4]

[1]Consultant, Psychiatric Social Worker, DMHP, Rohtas (District Hospital, SASARAM), Bihar
[2]Assistant Professor, Dept. of Cl. Psychology, Nayi Subah Institute of Mental Health, Varanasi
[3]Consultant, Clinical Psychology, DMHP, Rohtas (District Hospital, SASARAM), Bihar
[4]Consultant, Psychiatrist, DMHP, Rohtas (District Hospital, SASARAM), Bihar
Email: upendrasingh.aims@gmail.com

Background: Mental retardation currently also known as Intellectual Disability; is characterized by below-average intellectual or mental ability and a lack of skills necessary for day-to-day living. Care givers of person with intellectual disabilities experience many situations in day to day life. They experienced high level of financial, emotional and physical stress. Burden is one of the most conditions faced by families having intellectual disabled child. Aim: To know the level of burden on care givers of male and female with intellectual disability at Sasaram. Methodology: Cross sectional hospital based study. Purposive sampling method was adopted to collect data from 98 respondents at out Patient department of District Mental Health Program Unit, District Hospital, Sasaram, Bihar. After taking written consent structured socio-demographic data sheet, DST, VSMS, SFBT used for screening and Family burden Interview Schedule was administered. Result: Result of the present study show that burden experienced by the family in various aspect family routine burden, financial burden and mental health burden were highly significant. Conclusion: Family is primary support system of the person living with intellectual disability in our community. Care givers experience physical, economical, emotional, and personal burden while caring the disabled child.

Keywords: Family, Intellectual Disability, Caregivers, Burden.

Caregivers Challenges of Hospitalized Elderly

Ushvinder Kaur Popli[1], Rishi Panday[2]

[1]Professor & Head, [2]Ph.D. Scholar,
Department of Social Work, Jamia Millia Islamia, New Delhi. Email: rishiraj.lu@gmail.com

Background: Now a day every one busy his own life so caring of elderly is big challenge for caregivers. Care givers of hospitalized elderly experienced many problems during the care giving of elderly in hospital. They always worry about caring of elderly so take all responsibility of elderly them self. During care giving day by day care giver started to avoid his health care, family responsibility, job as well as social interaction with friends, neighbours and relatives. They do not participate in any social gathering and postpone or cancelled family activities like watching movie, holiday tour, marriage ceremony etc. Some time they do not celebrate any festival with family or friends because they engage in caring of elderly in hospital. Aim of the study: To study the caregiver challenges among caregivers of hospitalized elderly. Methods and materials: Descriptive research design used for this study and 30 care givers of hospitalized elderly from various hospitals in Delhi were selected through purposive sampling technique. Conclusion: Caregivers of hospitalized elderly face many obstacles in their personal life at the same time as demands of family including child rearing, career along with maintaining relationships with friends, neighbours and relatives. Due to care giving, care givers are suffering these types of problems as burden, stress, depression, irritability, aggression and variety of health complications.

Keywords: Caregiver burden, Care giver, Hospitalized Elderly.

Rashtriya Swasthya Bima Yojana Policy Planning and Implementation: A Comparison between Kerala and Madhya Pradesh State

Usman Khan

Research Scholar, TISS, Mumbai Email: usman.ahmad@tiss.edu

Introduction: A large chunk of poor people either borrow money or sell their asset to get access to health care facility in case any health emergency. Rashtriya Swasthya BimaYojana (RSBY) is seen as a way to protect these people from catastrophic health expenditure and overcoming their financial issues. In this paper, the researcher presents the debate on health insurance, the right to health, and universal health coverage (UHC). Then the paper moves to the RSBY scheme which is a public health insurance policy of India and traces the benefits under the policy. The paper discusses how the RSBY policy evolved and came into existence through Kingdon's theoretical framework of three streams. Lastly, a comparison in the implementation of the policy is presented between two states of India that is Kerala and Madhya Pradesh. Kerala is the best-performing state while Madhya Pradesh is the worst performing state as far as the implementation of the RSBY policy is concerned. The researcher attempted and felt the need for the study mainly to look at what worked well and critical success factors in Kerala, and on the other hand why the same policy failed in Madhya Pradesh State. Lastly, the researcher has mentioned how the policy has been modified by different state governments to increase the provisions under the policy and to reach out to the broader population for its optimum utilization. The Data and Findings: This article is based on secondary literature and data available on the website of the RSBY for Madhya Pradesh and Kerala State. The RSBY policy has been implemented in 10 districts of Madhya Pradesh and all 14 districts of Kerala with an average enrollment of 51.10% and 91.01% respectively. The total number of hospital needs to be impaneled in Madhya Pradesh are 422, out of which 81 are public and rest 341 are private. However, total numbers of hospitals impaneled were 166 only; out of which 81 are public and rest 85 are private. A significant difference can be observed in Madhya Pradesh state as far as the number of claims raised by hospitals is concerned. The lowest amount of claim is being received in Datia district while the high amount of claim received in Bhopal, Gwalior and Guna district. The claim ratio and burn out ratio is almost same in both the state. This is the beauty of the scheme that beneficiaries can utilize the benefits of the policy not only in any district of the state but any part of the country where empanelled hospital are available. The premium amount in Kerala is Rs. 738/- which is more than double as compared to Madhya Pradesh (Rs. 307/- in Madhya Pradesh). This is acting as a motivation for the insurance company to perform all activities efficiently in Kerala while low premium in Madhya Pradesh led to the cut down of critical activities.

Keywords: Health Insurance, RSBY, Social Security, Universal Health

The Role and Responsibility of Psychiatric Social work in Promotional Aspects of Health

Urvashi

Assistant Professor, Dept. of Social Work, C.S.J.M.U, Kanpur.
Email: urvashimsw88@gmail.com

Psychiatric social work is a specialization of social work that involves supporting, providing therapy to, and coordinating the care of individuals who are severely mentally ill and who require hospitalization or other types of intensive psychiatric help. Psychiatric social workers complete a variety of tasks when working with clients, including but not limited to psychosocial and risk assessments, individualized and group psychotherapy, crisis intervention and support, care coordination, and discharge planning services. Psychiatric social workers are employed in a wide range of settings, ranging from intensive inpatient wards to outpatient psychiatric clinics. Psychiatric social work is a challenging and very demanding profession. Social workers in this field must work closely with individuals suffering from complex and hard to manage conditions, who are in deep emotional distress and/or who may be a danger to themselves or others. Psychiatric social workers may also encounter difficulties in getting clients the resources and support they need to fully address their problems. However, some individuals gravitate to this work for its constant intellectual and professional challenges, and for the opportunity to help deeply vulnerable populations."Biomedical knowledge is essential for providing sound medical care, but it is not sufficient. The nature of dysfunctions and the physicians' transaction with the patient must also be informed by the psychosocial understanding. "Neither the mindless nor the brainless can be tolerated in medicine" (Lean Eisenberg, 2000). This statement is a quotation from the editorial address of the British Journal of Psychiatry as its entry into the 21st century. Eisenberg is one of the leading figures of psychiatry. Like other authoritative figures in medicine, L. Eisenherg found himself at the turn of the century, with the reality of integration. His statement clearly emphasizes the importance of integrating the biomedical, behavioral and psychosocial sciences in understanding the way the brain and the mind work and interact to generate normality or abnormality. In this integrative approach, clinical health psychology must play a significant role. Unfortunately, for many professionals in the medical field, this role is unclear.

Keywords: Role, Responsibilities, Psychiatric Social Work, Health

Breastfeeding and Health outcomes for Infant: A study conducted in slum area of Lucknow city

Vijai Sharma

Medical Social Worker, Department of Community Medicine, SPH, PGIMER, Chandigarh
Email: vijaimphill@gmail.com

It is a fact that breastfeeding saves the infant's live and also reduces their disease burden. Mother's knowledge about Breastfeeding helps to to improve breastfeeding and reduce the chances of disease. The new Sustainable Development Goals (2030), which build upon the MDGs. The achievement of all of these can be facilitated by improvements in breastfeeding. Breast feeding is beneficial for our children's immediate health and also subsequent adult health. Despite consolidation of evidence for breastfeeding's benefits in recent years, global action has stalled. There is a need for effective strategies. The benefits of breastfeeding are still under-recognized in many countries. Globally, less than half of newborns were breastfed within the first hour of birth and only 39% of children were breastfed exclusively for the first six months. Breastfeeding lays the foundation for good health, however global breastfeeding rates have remained stagnant for the past two decades. This research paper focuses upon breastfeeding practices and the health outcomes for infant. Present study has been conducted in slum area of Lucknow city. Purposive sampling technique was used for determining sample. 200 mothers were participate as respondent who had one year neonate. The results of this study provide knowledge of correct practice of breastfeeding among mothers and better health outcomes for infant.

Keyword: Infant, Mother's knowledge, Breastfeeding.

Psychosocial Rehabilitation in Mental Health

Chandrabala

MSW, Dept. of Psychiatry, GMCH, Chandigarh. Email: cbmankotia@gmail.com

Psychiatric rehabilitation ensure that persons with psychiatric disability can perform those cognitive , emotional, social, intellectual and physical skills needed to live, learn , work and function as normally and independently as possible in the community of their choice.

Individuals with mental illness (MI) have to suffer the depressing symptoms of their illness and unable to participate in their work and leisure activities (Primary disability). The illness is chronic in nature and recurrent and causes education and vocational training delay and discontinued (secondary Disability). Social factors like discrimination and stigma prevent people with mental health problem from giving employment (tertiary disability). Psychiatric rehabilitation or (psycho-social rehabilitation) enables persons with MI to develop to the fullest extent of their capacities despite the existence of mental illness. Psycho -social intervention is a process that deals with a broad range of psycho- social problems and promotes the restoration of social cognition And infrastructure as well as the independence and dignity of individual and groups. It serves to prevent pathological development and further social dislocation. The main techniques of psycho-social intervention are helping the individual, ventilating their emotion, active listening, showing empathy, helping them to externalize their interest, building the social support. The intervention should be holistic because it means emotional support and also practical help, suggestions, guidance, providing information and education. The focus is on the identification of needs and attention to specific problems related to areas like medical facility, legal aid, lively hood, housing etc. psychosocial intervention is done by using all the methods, techniques and skills of Psychiatric- social work that includes patient education, supportive therapy, group intervention, family intervention, breaking bad news, community re entry training , addressing disability benefit, unknown patients services, pre-discharge counseling, and rehabilitation.

Keywords: Psychosocial Rehabilitation, Mental Health

Social Medicine and Social Sciences

Jagpreet Singh

MSW, Dept. of Community Medicine, GMCH, Chandigarh.
Email: jagpreetmatta14@gmail.com

This paper is describing the manner in which disease may cause from, social problems and how public health or social medicine efforts may contribute to their solution.

Objective of Social Medicine: Identify social determinants of health and disease

- Devise mechanisms for alleviating suffering and ill health through social policies and action.
- Social, cultural, psychological and behavioral factors are important variables in the etiology, prevalence and distribution of disease.
- The way the people live, their habits, beliefs, values and customs are significant determinants of individual and collective health.
- The behavioral sciences have made significant role in developing better understanding about the social etiology of health problems.
- Sociology, Social Psychology, Cultural Anthropology.

Keywords: Social Medicine. Social Sciences

Study on Impact of Counseling Interventions with Multi Drug-Resistant Tuberculosis Patients

Amandeep Singh[1], Manjit Kaur[2]

[1]Research Scholar, [2]Research Associate

Social work is a profession primarily concerned with the remedy to psycho-social problems and deficiencies which exists in the relationship between the individual and his social environment. TB1 is one of among the major health problem, which has been killed number of lives in history and also effecting current health conditions, worldwide. This infection has a close relationship with immune system and people with low immunity are in more risk. The symptoms of active TB of the lung are coughing, sometimes with sputum or blood, chest pains, weakness, weight loss, fever and night sweats are common among all its types. MDR-TB2 infection may be classified as either primary or acquired. Primary MDR-TB occurs in patients who have not previously been infected with TB but who become infected with a strain that is resistant to treatment. Treatment for MDR-TB is long and carries significant side effects that make treatment adherence difficult for the patients. Though the WHO3 has recommended a shorter treatment regimen4 for MDR-TB, patients in India are still being treated under the previous regimen, which can last up to 24 months. The first six to nine months of treatment are particularly intensive, with the patient requiring daily injections and up to 13 tablets a day. People MDR-TB in low-income countries face many problems during treatment and cure rates are low. The purpose of the study was to identify and document the problems experienced by peoples receiving care for MDR-TB and how they cope when support is not provided, to estimate the effectiveness of counselling on treatment. This study had focused on the impact of counselling given to patient with and after medicine. It is found that counseling is a tool which is very useful to make patients healthy & Socially- Economically Developed.

Keywords: Tuberculosis, Multi Drug Resistance, World Health Organization

Overview of Slum Intervention Programme

Gurpreet Singh[1], *Jagtar Singh[1], Priya Rani[1]

[1]Executive Members AAS Welfare Society, Punjab Email: jagtardamdiwal62@gmail.com

Aim of the present study is to explore the socio-economic issues faced by the slum dwellers in Malerkotla and see the efficacy of the solutions implemented with the help of local administration. It was an exploratory study and sample consisted of one person each from 100 consecutive households in the study area. Inclusion criteria included participants of any age, any gender and not having any severe physical disability. Households which were locked were not included in the survey. After obtaining the informed consent, survey questionnaire prepared by the researchers was administered. Data obtained were analysed qualitatively. To address the needs in the area of education, sanitation and cleanliness; enrolment of children dropped out of school, free medical camps, providing water tank, cleanliness drive and distribution of free clothes was done to deal with problem at hand.

Keywords: Slum Dwellers, Problems Faced, Intervention

Organising Committee would like to acknowledge the contribution

Perfect Opticals

Medical Mart India

Capri Inc.

Dr. Duggals Dental Care Clinic Laser and Implant Center

Lion Lalit Behal,
President, Lions C
Club Chandigarh Central

Mr. Rahul Mahajan
Horticulturist

Mrs. Priti Rai

Harbhajan Kaur

www.ingramcontent.com/pod-product-compliance
Lightning Source LLC
LaVergne TN
LVHW080556160826
845677LV00010B/1870

9798466790795